Praise for *Brian David Bruns*

"Cruise Confidential is a deliciously addictive read..."
- **Travel Channel**

"I found it absolutely hysterical!"
- **Today Show**

"This man has seen it all."
- **20/20**

"...Ship for Brains is a fine pick, not to be missed."
- **Midwest Book Review**

"I couldn't put it down."
- **Chicago Sun-Times**

"This is a very funny, behind-the-scenes exploration of a cruise ship."
- **Booklist**

"Bruns doesn't hold back..."
- **Thomas Cook Magazine (UK)**

Cover design by Brian David Bruns

Interior layout by Steven Urban

Library of Congress Cataloguing-in-Publication Data

Bruns, Brian David

1st ed.

ISBN (print edition): 978-0-9856635-1-3
LCCN (PCN): 2013934033

1. Travel/Essay 2. Cycling—Humor 3. Travel—Iowa

DEDICATION

This book is dedicated to all the men and women, past and present, of the United States armed forces.

Though a proud member of the Civil War Trust—preserving the battlegrounds where our forefathers fought and died—I don't spend nearly enough time thinking about such men and women of *today*. I tend to focus on our innovators and entrepreneurs, our scientists, rather than the unsung heroes who preserve it all. This, despite the armed forces directly influencing my life. My father wasn't born a business professional and civic officeholder, after all, but four years of service in the Navy made it possible.

While writing this book I was reminded that my friend 'Aaron's' father was similarly catapulted to success by the military. 'Doc Owen' gave sixteen-some years of his professional life as an Air Force doctor. There he met Aaron's mother, the lovely Air Force nurse Barbara—herself a Navy brat and daughter of a highly decorated career sailor. And then, of course, there's Cheek: I still don't know what you do, never will, and don't care. I sleep better knowing you're on it.

This book is a hearty and overdue thank you.

ACKNOWLEDGMENTS

I would like to acknowledge the tens of thousands of annual riders and supporters of RAGBRAI for being awesome.

More specifically, however, I owe a great deal to the enthusiasm and assistance of the following friends and colleagues who helped make *Rumble Yell* a reality. To my excellent friends Matt and Rachael, John and Barbara: I can't thank you enough for being serendipitously present in various parts of the globe right when I needed you. Stephanie and Marc, a gracious thank you for exactly the same. I also wish to thank the reading prowess and enthusiasm of Sylvia and Brian Gilbert, as well as my editor, Geoff Hoesch. Kudos also go to Ben Woodbury of Paceline Products, who graciously helped sponsor the Chamois Butt'r campaign. Crotch lube all around!

Above all I thank my lovely wife Aurelia. None of this happens without your support and, perhaps more importantly, your patience. I love you!

TABLE OF CONTENTS

Rumble Strip

rum·ble [**ruhm**-b*uh*l] strip [**strip**]

noun

1. One of a series of rough or slightly raised strips of pavement on a highway, intended to slow down the speed of vehicles.

2. A Department of Transportation (DOT) study notes: "It is recognized that bicyclists cannot operate on roads or shoulders of roads with rumble strips." [2003]

3. While ignoring countless protests from bicycle advocates, a Michigan county caved to the local Amish lobby demanding they remove a new $20,000 rumble strip installation. Justifying removal costs estimated at $275,000 of taxpayer money, the DOT said they were not removing the strips just to appease the Amish. "The greatest safety concern [regarding rumble strips] for automobile drivers is avoiding horses jumping on the road." Cyclist safety issues were not discussed.

CHAPTER ONE

The Challenges

Why this place was chosen for 119 nuclear blasts was self-evident. Why I chose it for a bike ride was less clear. I was two hours away from the most revolting experience of my life, and I had no way of knowing it; a moment more awful than the 130° heat, more distressing than being alone in two million acres of utter waste. The nearest shade—a port-a-potty steaming in the sun—was twenty miles away. Getting there required a two-hour slog over desolate mountain ridges in unrelieved sun, on a bicycle so hot its metal burned any flesh unfortunate enough to touch it. My hands smarted even through gloves. No cars had passed this spot in days, barring a solitary DNR truck at 4AM. This I knew because I was already here in this horrible place. The truck's passage left a dead jackrabbit smashed upon the scalding asphalt at mile marker 33. Ravens circled above. They wanted me to leave. *I* wanted to leave.

But not before the most revolting experience of my life.

Training for the world's oldest, largest, and longest annual bike ride required some sacrifice. It was 500 miles of heat and hills and roadkill. Yet contrary to expectation, this greatest of Earth's bike touring tradition was not across the Sahara Desert, Australian Outback, or even somewhere in Europe. It was through America's heartland. I was training for RAGBRAI: *Register's Annual Great Bike Ride Across Iowa*. That's right: Iowa.

I wasn't doing this for glory—one rarely associates glory with Iowa—nor, as seemed more likely, was this some form of self-flagellation. This was to reconnect with an old friend I hadn't seen in twenty years. Aaron was a fascinating guy. Barring a penchant for wearing kilts and a need for corrective lenses, he was the living incarnation of Indiana Jones. Any opportunity to converse with such a man was worth some effort, and to rekindle an old friendship was even better.

I rubbed the grit from my eyes and squinted to the heat-wavering horizon. He better be worth it!

I am not a bicyclist by nature. I hadn't ridden one since my youth, which was a depressing number of decades ago. When Aaron suggested riding RAGBRAI, I said yes before actually thinking it through. Fortunately I was fit, but in other areas entirely, like running or dodging household objects occasionally thrown by my wife. If I was going to safely ride 500 miles, it required planning. Training. Oh, and a bike. I needed one of those.

How does one plan for such a monumental ride? Fortunately, RAGBRAI wasn't America's biggest bike ride without a great body of knowledge to draw upon. The official website was loaded with advice, including a calendar of recommended training rides. In fact, mercifully little thought would be required. Just follow directions to avoid injury. Being married, I was well versed in following directions to avoid injury.

So training I could do. 1,000 advance miles? Twas nothing. Buying all the gear from scratch? Ha! Credit cards. This was looking easier by the minute. But there was one great challenge I feared unsurmountable. No, not the heat of my home in Las Vegas, nor even finding *time* for 1,000 training miles therein. Something far, far more difficult awaited me: getting permission from my wife.

How to broach this adventure for the boys? Rare is the man who knows what women want to hear. This was compounded for me because my dear Aurelia was foreign. She grew up in the humble Romanian countryside but abandoned home for the action of the capital city. The result was a woman of ambition and self-reliance tempered by a natural shyness and her culture's enforced passivity in women. I just never knew when and where she would make a stand.

But what *really* made connection difficult, far more than her having lived under the Iron Curtain, was English. It was her third language and entirely self-taught by listening to hip hop music. Emigrating to Las Vegas did nothing to help get rid of her... colorful... phraseology. While I applauded Aurelia continually on this amazing feat of self-instruction, inwardly I cringed during even regular conversation. Her way of ordering me to the gym, for example, was by saying, "Junk in your trunk means no hoes 4 U."

Thus it was to this fitful little volcano I need explain my desire of riding RAGBRAI across my native state. Did I appeal to the fond pastoral memories of her youth, or work the 'everybody's doing it/hip today' angle? In the end I selected a different approach altogether. I decided to make it all about me. Dangerous? To be sure. Foolish? No doubt. But it was honest. That had to count for something.

Thus I expounded upon how completing RAGBRAI was every Iowan's rite of passage, a quantifiable method of proving our worthiness of that greatest of honors: being Iowan. We're a proud, hardworking folk, I exclaimed, getting positively worked up over the awesomeness of laboring 500 miles over 'amber waves of grain'—Iowa's lack of wheat fields notwithstanding—until I began singing the national anthem. This did not improve my argument.

"You want that for *vacation*?" Aurelia squeaked dubiously in her mousy voice. "Imma be in Hawaii. That's America, too."

"Come on, you've been to Iowa to see family..." I began.

"Chillaxin' with ya homies is different," she

replied. "Doncha wanna go somewhere interesting?"

"So you think Iowa's not worthy?" I chided.

Alas, Aurelia had a point. Did I really want to spend my vacation in Iowa? I was *from* Iowa, what more was there to see? After twenty-five years there, surely I'd seen it all—or all I wanted to, anyway. Since this wasn't about family, what on Earth would take me there, after all the exotic places I'd seen as a travel writer? A friend, that's what.

"We went to Maui last year," I protested. "You forced me to drive all over the island so you could see each and every beach, each and every town, each and every palm tree! I chauffeured you ten hours a day, every day. It was the most exhausting vacation I've ever had."

"And biking 500 kilometers is chill?"

"Miles," I corrected reflexively. "They're a lot longer than kilometers."

She batted her pretty eyelashes at me, revealing to my slow wits that I had just blundered into a trap.

"But... but... old people do it!" I blurted, desperate. "I mean retirees and stuff."

"Then bag her when you're old," she said, wiggling figure settling into a firm stance.

"There's pie," I tried.

"No pie," she said. "Denied!"

Unfortunately Aurelia also loved Suze Orman's TV show. She delighted in the long list of callers asking Suze's advice, such as, "I'm worth $1.3 Million. Can I buy a new Prius?" Suze's answer never varied: *denied!* Aurelia's tiny voice somehow only underscored the finality of the word. But I had an ace up my sleeve. One of Iowa's triumphs was Aurelia's Achilles heel.

"They have pork."

She paused.

"Old school pork," I pressed on, sensing my advantage. "Heaps of it. Iowa pork chops are over a pound each, baby."

Despite my dinky wife's utter lack of body fat, she consumed vast amounts of pork. One might say freakish amounts of pork. Her metabolism was hyperactive, like that of a small mammal, and she regularly snarfed down more food than I, an active man double her weight. Further, she went straight for the heavy stuff. No lean tenderloins for her, oh no. Growing up in rural Romania she learned to dunk hunks of pork into barrels of bubbling, rendered pork fat. With salt. They ate entire slabs of smoked fat called *slanina*, sometimes mixing it with eggs but more often popping it straight into their mouths. With salt. While American bacon was little meat and lots of fat, Romanian bacon abandoned the idea of meat altogether. But had lots of salt.

"Iowa has the best pork in the country," I continued. "It's glorious, I tell you, glorious! Our pigs live the high life. I can bring some home."

"When you leaving?"

Of course Aurelia encouraged rekindling my friendship with an old high school buddy. Though Romanian, she wasn't a witch. But that didn't mean she gave me carte blanche, either. I was under strict orders to manage the budget such that Hawaii was still available later. I happily informed her that RAGBRAI meant camping, so the only cost was reasonably-priced vendor food all week. Oh, and transportation to Iowa. And buying a bike. And *its* transportation to Iowa. And, um, gear, like jerseys and bike shorts and a helmet. And a tire pump. And energy bars. Icy Hot? I was talking myself into a hole.

So my first task was to buy equipment under the intense scrutiny of an Iron Curtain Suze Orman. *Denied!* We had radically different views on the value of the US dollar. This was a good thing, because she kept me from frivolously wasting money on small items perhaps more expensive than need be. The downside was a complete denial of treats. "Snickers for $1.29? You know what that buys in Romania? Denied!"

I didn't know how much a new bike would cost, but figured it would surely cost more than the $200 Aurelia allocated for it. I protested, "I need to get something of fair quality. You expect me to ride safely for 1,500 miles on a bike that costs less than shoes you wear to a nightclub?"

"You said 500 miles," she countered.

"It's not just the ride," I pointed out, "it's also *training*. I'll probably need a grand for everything."

"*What?*" she squeaked in outrage. "You think I'm made of Benjamins?"

"You paid $500 for a leather coat you've never worn," I protested. "And never will, 'cause this is *Las Vegas*. Hello? It's hot here."

At least the leather coat made a good blanket for

my night on the couch.

There were five bike shops in Las Vegas. We visited them all, with increasingly maddening results. Only two offered a 'cheap' bike for $3000. I refused to believe that bikes cost that much when something like 40% of Las Vegas homes had mortgages underwater. But compared to prices closer to the Strip, these were bargains.

Finally we went to the Schwinn dealer. I grew up with Schwinn bikes and knew they weren't titanium-alloy or whatever Schwarzenegger's *Terminator* was made of. The show floor was very wide and open, a refreshing change from the crowded boutique-style shops Vegas preferred. After having already wasted hours in fruitless searching, we wasted no more and marched right up to the counter. There waited a man of perhaps sixty, wearing a sweater and sporting a mustache. He looked very professorial.

"Good afternoon," I said. "I would like to see the bikes you have under $1,000."

"Certainly," he said, moving around the counter. We walked down row upon row of bicycles and he pointed out numerous delicate plastic and aluminum pink things with ribbons and stuff for little girls.

"I'm sorry," I clarified. "I meant for me. I'm doing a 500-mile ride."

He laughed. I couldn't believe it. He *laughed* at a customer!

"People in Vegas sure are dreamers," he said, snuffling back more chuckles, "But really, come on."

This from a sixty-something guy? Didn't he recall

a different world than post-building nuthouse Vegas? I began to fear my visions of a perfect vacation by immersing myself into Midwestern wholesomeness as likely as meeting Elvis. OK, bad example.

Finally we found a mom and pop store we liked. The couple was extremely young, but the moniker still fit. Both were dubious of such a 'cheap' bike, but offered to try. Most likely they wanted to get their hooks into fresh meat. Using catalogues the lady helped me select a bike for a 'piddly' $800.

"This will be a good starter bike," she said, or rather grudgingly admitted. "But before the year is out you'll want to upgrade to a real bike."

Her comment was so offhand as to be honest.

"The price includes a custom fit to your gait when it comes in. And we generously give away a free water bottle."

The indicated water bottle was crammed with their logo, address, email address, and QR code.

"Do you need all the gear, too?"

"Yes," I said, grimacing. I was right to cringe because the list of necessaries was extensive. But I got moderately priced equipment in the form of a portable tire repair kit—imperative when biking alone through Nevada's desert wastes—a tire pump, a helmet, a bike rack for the Jeep, and other miscellaneous odds and ends. I also opted for the heavy-duty lock, since we had been robbed eight times in our three years in Vegas.

"Say, can I order a bike seat that's bigger? These are all so small and hard."

"The big ones are soft and squishy for short

rides," she explained. "On long rides butts move around too much."

"But I have a little butt," I protested weakly. She looked dubious at this claim. Perhaps worse, Aurelia failed to contain a squeaking laugh.

"It's all about friction, you see," she continued. "Smaller surface area means less friction. You don't want friction down there."

"No, I don't think I do," I agreed. "So a tiny, rock-hard seat guarantees no friction?"

"Oh, no," she scoffed, laughing at the absurdity of the idea. "There's no *guarantee* of anything. Why else do you think there's so many crotch lubes?"

"Crotch lubes?" Aurelia squawked. "Denied!"

The selection of crotch lubes was indeed impressive, not unlike the hair product aisle of a salon with dozens of tubes, tubs, and jars. I was mesmerized by the half-gallon vat of *Butt Butter*. I expected a broad selection of such things in this city, of course, but at the Adult Toy Emporium or any other of our 500-plus adult establishments.

Skipping the lubes for the moment, I instead loaded up on energy bars. Most were chocolate or yogurt-covered bars. At that early juncture, I didn't realize just how stupid it was to buy any of them. That would come back to haunt me. Like, four times a week for the next four months.

The morning after the arrival and fitting of my new bike, I pulled the Jeep into the garage and quietly unhitched the goods from the rear rack. Everything smelled of fresh rubber and crisp plastic. Aurelia tiptoed through the inside door wearing her robe. She looked tired but courteously pretended to be interested.

"I'm sorry I woke you," I apologized.

"Happy with your new toy?" she asked in a tiny, sleepy voice.

"My new *tool*, woman," I corrected with feigned machismo. "I'm sure it pales in comparison with Aaron's bike, but that's OK. As long as it keeps me up with him."

Aurelia yawned. She worked nights as a roulette dealer on the Strip, so I didn't drain her further by expounding upon my excitement over the bike. I did, however, wax poetic over the reason for it.

"You'd like Aaron, you know," I said, leaning over the bike to engage her. "He and his wife Isabel are world travelers. Can you believe they just flew to Argentina to tour wineries and stay with friends? Yes, they somehow have friends in Argentina, unlike the rest of us mere mortals."

To my surprise, Aurelia groaned.

"What?" I asked, suddenly defensive.

"So they're bottles in the club?"

I just stared at her, waiting for an explanation of how people could be bottles in a club.

"You know, spending crazy money on bottle service just to show off. Who goes to Argentina to tour wineries? Go to California."

"Oh, it's nothing like that," I reassured her, "Aaron's a true traveler."

I launched into my best narrator's voice. "No mere collector of refrigerator magnets, he. Aaron is a man who takes the best of other cultures and integrates them into his life. To be sure, his latest example of cultural fusion was downright shocking. For he is a Portlander through and through, which means not only a love of coffee, but an obsession, a mania! He's a monster. Bereft of caffeine, he's the terror of co-workers and small children. Yet after spending a month in Hungary—yes, he's done that, too —he discovered that simple, strong peasant tea suited his stomach better. So back to America he went, and off of coffee he got. Now he drinks tea. His peers call him un-American, but I say it makes him the ultimate American: we're the Melting Pot, are we not? No, I declare Aaron Owen is no bottle on the shelf!"

Aurelia blinked and wavered, having apparently fallen asleep again during my droning. Rousing, she asked, "You done?"

"Yeah," I mumbled. "Sorry."

"It's bottle in the *club*," she corrected, stifling a giggle. "But really, you haven't seen him in twenty years. What are you hoping for?"

"That he doesn't wear a kilt," I said. "He's very proud of his English ancestry."

Aurelia giggled and sang, "Everybody in the house, *represent!*"

"You mean represent Las Vegas?" I said, aghast at the notion. "What, wear sequins and bushy sideburns? No way."

"So he's from England?"

"No, but both sides of his family are. His mother traced her lineage back to like the 1300s or something crazy like that. He did attend some college in Nottingham, though."

"Oh, wait," Aurelia exclaimed. "He's that Indiana Jones friend of yours!"

"That's right," I said. "He did an archeological dig in Israel during college. He's also toured the ruins of Machu Picchu and who knows what else."

"So they're rich."

"I don't think so," I said, frowning in thought. "Well, his *parents* are loaded. His dad's like some genius radiologist. I was always really impressed with how they handled their money. They refused to spoil their kids with stuff, but spared no expense for expanding their world-views. Aaron was smart enough to take advantage of the opportunities his parents gave him. True, he was lost in college for years trying to figure out what he wanted to do with his life. Too many options, I guess. His emails are more about being a Portlander than his job, so I don't know what he ended up doing. I think it has something to do with urban development."

"You'll find out in July."

"Indeed I will!" I exclaimed, patting the seat of my new bike. I frowned at how distressingly hard it felt.

Though very impressed with Aaron's world travels, I actually felt ever so slightly on par with them. Luckily, I had been around, too. When I neared thirty, fate stuck her nose into my life in the form of an exotic foreign woman. I was hopelessly—some would say pathetically—smitten and followed her everywhere. In her case that meant further afield than just her native Romania, but also the Caribbean, Mediterranean, and Baltic. Cruise ships were our vehicle, but not as passengers. Oh no: we worked on them, slaving ten months on, two months off. But those two months were free and clear, allowing travel to a variety of other cultures. It was an exciting life, but an exhausting one. After four years the time came to return to land. The question was where to make our fortune? Vegas, baby!

It was all about Aurelia, of course. She was a quad-lingual roulette dealer who had worked in multiple nations before joining ships, and she was pretty. That was a recipe for success. Within a year she had ascended to the best casino on the Las Vegas Strip. A good thing, too, because as a writer my income amounted to little more than a tax write-off. So Las Vegas was good to us, even if we didn't care for living there. But if there was anything I had learned in my travels, it was that every place was worthy unto itself. To think otherwise was simply ethnocentrism.

Thus, I was quite excited to return to Iowa and explore. Growing up in Cedar Rapids, one of the few *relatively* large cities in Iowa, I had seen no reason to visit tiny farming communities hours away in the far corners of the state. What starry-eyed teen would? So I did not necessarily know my own state. Now I had a chance to see it slowly, fully. Perhaps only now that I was older and wiser could I truly value the merits of small town USA. It was a shame Aurelia would not join me, but an athlete she most certainly was not, nor a camper.

Ah, but it turned out camping would not be so necessary! Aaron informed me that his father had volunteered to drive our support vehicle. This was more than just some guy driving a van full of tents and extra clothes: Doc was bringing a 42-foot RV!

While Aaron and his travels did not necessarily humble me, his father was another matter. Doc was a staggeringly intelligent and insightful man. Further, he was one of the bravest, yet most pragmatic men I knew. He asked the hard questions of life and the world and was not afraid of the answers he found, nor afraid to voice them. Yet this man was no dusty, boring intellect. Doc was a charming, patient conversationalist with a great sense of humor—and a 42-foot RV!

Doc was a world traveler, too, despite humble beginnings as a minister's son. He joined the Air Force and there became a doctor. Of immensely more importance, he also met his best friend and wife Barbara. After their military career they retired to Cedar Rapids, where Doc reinforced his already impressive medical credentials to become a leading radiologist in Eastern Iowa. They also started a family. Though I didn't even meet Aaron until our high school years, I was all but welcomed into their family as an honorary member. This made me exceedingly proud. Over the years their enthusiasm and support had never wavered.

It was shaping up to be a perfect vacation. A perfect opportunity to catch up with an old friend, with hours of quiet biking through gentle countryside. A perfect place to relax after a hard ride, with real showers instead of car washes and a perfect night's sleep in air-conditioned comfort. A perfect reunion. Perfect everything.

But one simply cannot just show up for a 500-mile ride. Training must come first. And my RAGBRAI training was far, far from perfect.

CHAPTER TWO

Training on Planet Vegas

I don't know what normal is, but I know what normal is not. Normal is not Las Vegas. This is fundamental to the city, for who goes there to do what they normally do? Las Vegas exists to zipline naked over gyrating topless dancers throwing money at you. That just doesn't happen in normal life. At least not mine.

Nor is the location of Las Vegas normal. Humans were not meant to live there. Nor did they—until us foolish white folks, that is. The Native Americans of the area, the Southern Paiutes, Hualapai, and others, preferred the nearby rocks of Valley of Fire. Yes, they actually preferred living in a place called *Valley of Fire* to Las Vegas. That fact alone spoke volumes.

But live there I did, and training I needed. Aaron biked daily in Portland, and if our time together was going to be perfect, I needed to keep up with him! I began to obsess over training. First came rides around my neighborhood. It seemed an excellent way to start because I could keep the rides short but worthy, because we lived in mountain foothills with some tough inclines. But I had to do a lot more than just thirty minutes during lunch, or an hour after work. I had to do some pretty big rides. I needed rides over fifty miles, even up to eighty. That meant exiting the city, and that meant hostile terrain.

For my first trip into the wild I selected the Red Rock Canyon Scenic Byway. This was actually right next to the city sprawl—beginning at Red Rock Casino and Spa, of course—so I was not too terribly far from civilization should things go awry. I was excited to see how my new bike handled the untamed undulations of tectonic madness that created the candy-striped Rainbow Escarpment and cherry-red upthrusts of Red Rock Canyon. Lonely country, indeed, but simply gorgeous. The bike worked great for being so 'cheap'. I began hitting that route several times a week, gleefully inching up the mileage each time. A month passed and the heat level rose. It soon became the defining issue of each ride. But I persevered for adventure, for Aaron, for me.

The time came for a big ride. A thirty miler on the Scenic Byway would max out the loop. I was eager to conquer that road. But most of all, I was eager to plumb that greatest biking mystery of all. For, unbeknownst to my dear Aurelia, I had secretly bought some crotch lube. Even more secretly—so secret I didn't dare admit it even to myself—I was excited to try it. I didn't exactly know why chamois cream intrigued me so, but I was eager to find out.

A chamois was simply the name for the cushion built into biking-specific shorts: a big, smooth pad in the crotch. Somehow, somewhere, lubricant was involved. I'd never before devoted time to exploration of this uniquely biking ritual. Though I had worn some pretty outlandish stuff—generally in the privacy of my own bedroom—this was a new one.

Chamois creams had exciting names. Vegas names. Most were anatomically-minded—as if deep down we aren't all anatomically-minded—like *Assos, DZ Nuts,* or *Butt Paste.* Others were playfully animalistic, such as *Udderly S-MOO-th.* Some combined both, a la *Bag Balm.* I'm not afraid to admit that *Beljum Hard Core Budder* intimidated me, as did the description for *Friction Freedom*: 'helps heal and manage existing saddle sores, while preventing chafing, and bacterial and fungal infections that cause hot spots and infections.' Did I really want to risk all *that* for Aaron, or any reason whatsoever? In the end I opted for the apparent leader of the pack, *Chamois Butt'r.* Even then I was scared because it came in little portable containers that looked distressingly like a suppository.

My first dilemma was figuring out if I wore underwear with the bike shorts or not. I decided in true American fashion that more is better, which meant if one layer was safe, two was safer. I wore underwear. Feeling exceedingly self-conscious, I squirted a bunch of *Chamois Butt'r* down there. Chafing even as I walked around the Jeep did not bode well.

Things immediately took a turn for the worse.

By mile six, I had to stop. This was a common turn around point for day-trippers as it was the location of a beautiful scenic overlook. I didn't stop to enjoy the gaping views of tectonic splendor and wildly diverse color, but rather to adjust my smarting crotch and answer nature.

It was hot outside, of course. Though only March, the sun already burned a good hundred degrees in the Mojave Desert. Heat waves bounced off the hard earth with more intensity than even from the highway's black asphalt. Crazy anything could grow in that dirt. Few things did, actually, and all were ornery as Hell. If something grew, it had spikes. If it didn't have spikes, it had hide thick as an elephant's. Supposedly, animals lived out there, burrowing things like lizards, kangaroo rats or jackrabbits. A rather vocal non-profit organization insisted this was the habitat of the endangered desert tortoise, but I didn't believe it. I had been hiking these wastes for years and hadn't seen a thing, including tracks. To this day I maintain that tortoises don't exist.

So, sweating and panting, I eased my aching ass off the bike and unbuckled my helmet. The straps dangled down my cheeks to scratch off the sunblock, but breathing came more easily. I stiffly proceeded to the toilets, keenly aware of suffering some sort of diaper rash. I couldn't remember the last time I had that, but was pretty sure it sucked then, too.

The facilities were merely pit latrines, if immaculately maintained. The concrete structure provided a measure of relief from the heat, but it was still more than hot enough to keep the pit's contents fresher than I cared to smell. I stood before the latrine and looked down to deal with the rather intimidating bike shorts. There was no fly in the chamois, of course, just soggy cloth and spandex stretched perversely across my privates, smashing them into forms no man ever wants to see. True, people probably paid for that in Vegas, but I was not one of them. I tried not to dwell on the fact that I was doing it to myself, for free, for Aaron. I leaned forward to get a better look at my brutalized package.

Mistake.

My helmet tumbled from my head, dropping directly into the latrine. The fall was a clean one, missing the rim entirely to plummet directly into the pit. It landed with a sickening, squishy thump. I blinked in disbelief, staring down at my new $65 helmet perched neatly atop a rising mound of feces. This was not good. This was distinctly bad. And I had twenty-four more miles to go!

Turns out head safety wasn't the problem. The problem was a wild burro attack. Yes, a wild burro attack. I sensed that maybe, just maybe, Aaron's training in Oregon presented less challenges for him. Bigfoot, maybe.

It happened at mile twenty. I had reached the end of the Scenic Byway and already turned back, pausing at a rather enchanting notch between mountains that obviously had a hidden water source somewhere. A few lonely willow trees rose up, but, confused and defeated, drooped back down to the rocky earth and rough scrub. It was the only roadside shade on the entire Scenic Byway, other than the manufactured overlook back at mile six.

Severely stiff and crotch blazing, I eased off my bike. Groaning, I awkwardly squatted to remove a snack from a seat bag on the bike. Progress was even more painfully slow than slogging up miles-long hills against thirty mile per hour winds. Finally I retrieved my treasure and grinned through sun-cracked lips.

The euphoria was short-lived. The energy bar was nothing more than a gooey mess, like a cookie pulled too soon from the oven. Grunting and still squatting like some sort of animal, I licked the hot gunk from the wrapper. I carefully forced out of my mind worries about training rides when summer hit. This was only early spring, after all.

I spied the burro half a mile away through the scrub brush, nuzzling a cholla. He spied me, too, and began noisily honking. The sound carried easily over the dead, scorched earth. He began trotting towards me until perhaps a hundred feet away. Then he charged.

Panic flashed through me. The burro moved incredibly fast. I could never outrun him—certainly not with a funky diaper rash—and I doubted I could start on my bike with anything approaching alacrity. I wasn't sure what to do. I considered briefly sitting down and crying, but sitting would hurt worse than anything the burro would do. So I frantically hobbled to a desert-willow and peeked around the trunk. At least that would break the wild beast's charge.

I never underestimated wild animals in Nevada, for I had been attacked by some pretty benign-seeming beasts. Once a horde of bunnies nearly ended my life. Yes, really. The worst, though, was being attacked by an angry stallion who thought I was chasing his fillies. That had been absolutely terrifying, seeing such a huge, magnificent animal overtly displaying aggressive behavior and me being several miles of cross-country running from my Jeep. I survived that, so there was nothing to worry about in a lousy mule, right?

Wrong.

The charging burro was easily an eight hundred pound wild animal. Many reached a thousand pounds. All were hardened survivors of the worst land nature had to offer. I had seen cute, fuzzy youngsters placidly snacking on cactus thorns the size of my fingers. I didn't want to mess with *anything* that had a mouth that tough. He could have bitten right through my helmet, if I still had one. I didn't even want to imagine a kick from those hooves.

The burro got about twenty feet away and slowed. Finally he stopped and eyed me. I eyed him back from behind the relative safety of the tree.

He appeared young because his coat was pretty and trim and he was slender. Most wild burros I'd seen had barrel chests and shaggy coats. His neck had a rough spot, as if something had tried to take him down. It looked exactly like a predator's mark, and it gleamed. Yes, that was blood. For sure it was. I didn't know what could take a chunk out of an animal that big, and I didn't want to find out. There were no big predators in the Mojave, unless you counted the aggregate mass of a coyote pack. That was unlikely, but not impossible.

The burro seemed content to just observe. Then he became vocal. He honked at me. Presumably he associated humans with food. I told him I didn't have anything to eat, which was true. He didn't believe me. Nor would he shut up about it. It's rare to find someone who talks more than me. And in the animal kingdom? You have to look for screaming monkeys and stuff. A long time passed, and he seemed in no hurry to leave. I, on the other hand, thought leaving most prudent.

But, simply put, I couldn't take any more chafing. I just couldn't. Squatting beneath the desert-willow, I stripped off my loathsome chamois. Decency was irrelevant as it was just the burro and me.

If only.

Suddenly, and for the first time in *hours*, cars appeared on the Scenic Byway. What were the odds they would pass at this one and only moment? But life could be mean like that. The cars whizzed by as my white, über-lubed butt glowed brilliantly from the shade of the tree. But removing my soggy underwear provided instant relief, and that mattered more than anything else. I smashed the squishy underwear into the bike satchel and oh-so-carefully remounted. I delicately rubbed my tender privates atop the bike saddle. Everything slid properly over the lubricated chamois. I sighed. The burro approved with a honk. I was glad he couldn't speak English.

All that was just a single thirty-mile ride! Of course, it got worse. Much, much worse.

But I learned. I learned that the proper and generous application of *Chamois Butt'r* prevented saddle sores. I learned that, as I've always maintained, underwear is just in the way. I also learned that sometimes Mom was right.

Like so many rebellious youths, I had scoffed when Mom told me drinking from the garden hose would cause a bacterial invasion that would devour my flesh and eat my brains. I did it anyway. I'm fine. I also scoffed when Mom told me that not wearing a hat would cause frost bite that would destroy my flesh and freeze my brains. Soon as she wasn't looking, off came the hat. Mom also told me to wear a helmet when riding my bike. Really, Mom. Just how uncool do you want your son to be?

But I learned that helmets *were* necessary. Very, very necessary.

I was beginning at the Red Rock Canyon Scenic Byway. A traffic light separated the parking lot from the desert road. I neared the traffic signal and slowed on the sidewalk, waiting for a green light. My bike wavered a bit, but my balance was good. My distance calibration needed some work, though. The handlebar met a pole and jerked the front wheel perpendicular to my forward momentum. In a blink I was falling backwards to the pavement. My head smacked onto the sidewalk with a thunderous CRACK!

I lay there a moment, seeing stars. I had never seen stars like that before. It defied credulity that my head hit so brutally hard. Damn you, physics! Whiplash... at three miles per hour! But while my bike was only moving slowly, my body had fallen much faster, with my head whipping down with crushing force. Had I not been wearing a helmet I would have been really and truly damaged. What followed was a rare moment of sobriety. And, of course, yet another trip to the store to buy yet another helmet.

So I learned to give it up to Mom on that one.

I also learned to hate Vegas cyclists.

Red Rock Canyon Scenic Byway. Saturday morning. 7AM. The parking lot was full. A long line of men and women in brilliant spandex jerseys snaked out of the Starbucks. Small clusters talked to each other, but that rarely meant meaningful conversation. Most merely waited for the other to stop talking so they could brag about their bike and gear.

I generally avoided the Scenic Byway on weekends because it was a favorite cruising destination for Las Vegans and tourists. The road rumbled with speeding Lamborghinis, Ferraris, and Harleys. Staying alive in all that meant sticking to the shoulder. After half an hour I passed the scenic stop with its helmet-eating latrine. The area was brimming with bicyclists already turning back. Go on, little riders, shell out

$3000 worth of bike, and another $1,000 worth of clothing, just to stop and turn around for only an hour ride. Go on, I say! These bikers were all show and no substance. I had faced a wild burro and survived! Go ahead, little people, discuss your expensive doodads at Starbucks. I'm busy being awesome.

Enter: rude awakening.

A block of riders overtook me, dominating the shoulder by riding double-wide, handlebar to handlebar. A single cyclist rode at the fore, like Death himself on a pale bike, leading the Riders of the Apocalypse. They numbered not four, but eleven: leader crying havoc before ten instruments of Armageddon, crushing and casting aside all in their path.

Exit: stage right.

Forced off the shoulder at top speed, I was nearly hurled into a rugged washout twenty feet deep. By sheer luck—and adrenaline—I managed to collapse instead of fly. Pain blasted through me as I hit the crumbling bank of rocks, sliding right up to the very edge. I felt each and every rock, but it was better than a similar crunch after a twenty-foot fall. The Hell riders zoomed past my head, a blur of snapping yellow jerseys and disdain, their cadence booming into desert, crossing the wastes and echoing off distant mountains.

"Who's Lance?"
"WE'RE LANCE!"
"Who's Lance?"
"WE'RE LANCE!"

"How many?"
"SEVEN!"
"How many?"
"SEVEN!"

Surely this wasn't what I was going to encounter on RAGBRAI: herds of Lance Armstrong wanna-bes? Only then did it occur to me I would be one of a *minimum* of 10,000 simultaneous riders. My vision blurred, only to refocus on recollections of one Tour de France rider falling and dozens of poor, following riders tumbling into him. I wasn't prepared for that at all!

But when things don't go your way in Vegas, nobody calls it quits. We double down. In my case, I swapped the Scenic Byway's thirty miles of all but lonely desert for the unlimited milage of freakin' aliens-only desert. Literally. I chose the wastes north of Las Vegas, mere miles from Area 51 and its supposed UFO sightings. This was a place so God-forsaken that the U.S. military continued to test top-secret stuff out there, knowing no normal human would ever dare go there. So for Aaron I risked getting abducted by aliens. Fortunately, no anal probes occurred. At that point my butt was so numb I probably wouldn't have noticed anyway. But something particularly loathsome did occur.

It was on my longest training ride, an eighty-five miler. I started the ride at 3:40AM. That didn't mean I woke up at 3:40, oh no. It was an hour drive just to get to my starting point. So up at 2:30 I was, knowing how bad the heat would get. Or I thought I did. You never really prepare yourself for heat pushing 130°, you just think you do.

I parked the Jeep on the side of the road at mile marker 1. It was still dark. Stars were visible to the north and west, but already fading into the rosy glow of the east. To the south lay Las Vegas, source of enough light to make the cosmos squint. This place was so awful that after 119 nuclear blasts the landscape hadn't noticeably changed. So they set off 500 more underground.

By flashlight I readied my hydration backpack with a forty-ounce bladder. Two ice packs were tucked within to keep it all relatively cool, for after a few hours in *that* heat water could brew tea. I brought some gel-like globules called Gu-Chomps, hoping to swallow the scalding hot mass they would inevitably become. For lunch I had a Pemmican-brand energy bar. This was carefully devoid of chocolate or yogurt or anything else that would melt. Thus my reward at halfway—43 miles!—was basically a sack of oats, fat, and sugar compressed into a bar. For you, Aaron.

I sprayed myself liberally with half a can of 50 SPF sunblock—an odd thing to do in the blackness of night—wet my lips with 50 SPF Chapstick, and was ready to go. Out there nature provided no shade whatsoever. Well, that wasn't entirely true. At mile fifty-something—beyond the turn-around point—was a stagnant oasis of crusty water laden with violent amoebas. There rose three sorry-looking trees and five signs warning the water was toxic.

Though starting in darkness, I wasn't worried about being struck by a car. My bike had been haphazardly painted Day-Glo green and would easily catch headlights. Who would drive out there at this hour anyway? At *any* hour? Only a single DNR truck forced to do so. I considered the solitude. The quiet of the desert was awesome, humbling, frightening. This was a rare place where man held no sway, but only left evidence of passage to elsewhere. Yet the silence was deeper than merely the absence of man. It was the rarified silence of no life at all. No plants to rustle, no crickets to chirp, no birds to cry. The ribbon of asphalt undulated alone across bone-dry washes and through barren mountains of exposed rock upthrust to reveal literally four billion years of past life. *Past* life.

Such a profound record of life's fecundity surrounded me. Where had it all gone? Why?

The answer rose presently. Sunlight crawled over the 'cool' 85° landscape with destroying heat, stirred brutally hot winds and lethal aridity. Out there people had been found dead with water still in their possession. The severe dryness sucked all moisture from their bodies faster than drinking could replenish it.

Another hour or so the thermometer registered 115°. Heat rebounding off the dead earth added uncharted degrees. Surprising, then, was encountering the first sight of life. Buzzards circled up ahead. No, not buzzards, but ravens: huge, black, and bigger than my fourteen-pound cats. I rode towards them, wondering for what they were waiting to die. But do not ask for whom the bell tolls: it tolls for thee. At mile marker 33 I passed a dead jackrabbit the size of a beagle. The poor creature was smashed, innards steaming in the sun. It freaked me out.

Just two hours later it would freak me out far, far more. But more on that later.

Over the course of four months of nearly constant riding, I discovered that I hated biking. It wasn't just the Vegas riders, though that was a big part of it. It wasn't even the heat, though that was an even bigger part of it. No, I loathed biking because my rides had almost universally been in winds ranging from twenty to thirty miles per hour—on a *good* day. Nothing broke the wind for hundreds of miles in all directions of Vegas, so gusts fanned out over the wastes to push you off the road and belittle your puniness of size and effort. When mountains interfered they made it worse, channeling the winds into tunnels that roared through the barren passes I labored through. Biking was not fun. It was torture.

But all that was done. The time had come to pack away the hateful skin-searing, crotch-killer. Dismembering the bike was a surprisingly satisfying experience. My victory was ultimately denied, however. The last pedal refused to come off. I struggled so mightily that I broke the ratchet! After a trip to the store and much profanity I resumed my effort, only to be continually defeated. Finally I just shoved the frame into the slender box, scraping the pedal down the side. It burst through the cardboard. With devilish glee I drew a band-aid over the area and added a cartoon-style bubble caption shouting "$@& %!"

But the drama wasn't done. The shipping company failed to arrive and pick up the wounded box. Because timing was critical in this step, I called them in a panic.

"You didn't pick up my parcel!" I cried into the phone. "It's gotta be shipped by today or it won't make it on time."

"Our apologies," replied a nasally man through the phone. "What is the address?"

"Shiny Skies Drive," I replied hastily.

"Chinese Guys Drive," the voice repeated. "Yes, my notes say they went there yesterday and found no package."

"Shiny Skies," I repeated with emphasis.

"Chinese Guys."

"*Skies*, man!" I burst out. "Isn't this Las Vegas? Clear *skies*, as in no clouds. The sun *shines* here all the damn time. *Shiny skies*."

"Of course, sir. Our apologies. We will send a truck to pick up your parcel at Chinese Guys Drive, in sunny Las Vegas. Thank you for your business."

Irrationally angry, I shoved the box into the Jeep and hauled it straight to the transport company's office. I was thrilled to get rid of the thing. I never wanted to see it again. But boy, would I. A week's worth of loathsome riding awaited.

Aaron better be worth it.

But rid of the toil of actual riding, and with the assistance of much rum, happy dreams of biking bubbled to the surface. I grew enthusiastic anew and began scouring the internet for bits and pieces of trivia or advice. Eventually I clicked on the official map of elevation. My jaw dropped.

RAGBRAI claimed that Day 1 had 4,298 feet of elevation gain over 59.5 miles. According to the source I had been training with, MapMyRIDE.com, the route only climbed 1,400 feet. RAGBRAI was going to be *66% harder* than I thought. In fact, Day 1 and Day 2 were *both* harder than *any* single day of Colorado's famed Ride the Rockies! Though the latter crested several mountain passes, its total elevation gain only beat RAGBRAI by 400 measly feet.

I tried to calm myself. I knew this. I was raised in Iowa. Everyone not from Iowa stereotyped it as flat as a pancake. Such riders faced one hell of a learning curve! There are easily eighty rivers in Iowa, with each and every one carving its own valley—a valley to pedal out of. Then, of course, there were the two monsters bordering the state: the Muddy Missouri and the Mighty Mississippi. 10,000 years ago the glaciers receded and let those bad boys loose. Since then they've wreaked havoc unchecked, carving and moving and carving again. And carving power did they have: the Mississippi alone tapped a whopping thirty-two American states and two Canadian provinces to make the fourth greatest drainage on the planet.

None of it mattered. It was too late to chicken out. Like it or not, I was going to Iowa!

Saturday, July 23rd. Glenwood, Iowa. Such was the date and place, one day prior to the celebrated tire dip. The Midwest's largest bike expo—take *that*, Chicago—was set up in the parking lot of the Glenwood Community High School. After goodbye hugs from my shuttling parents—and Mom's last minute check that I had a helmet—I said goodbye, shouldered my week's worth of gear, and strode down to the sprawling series of tents, canopies, and kiosks.

Aaron had texted me to meet him at the bike delivery area. For some reason cell phone reception was spotty in Glenwood, but the message squeaked through. Finding the appropriate tents among the many presented no challenge, as the dozens of slender boxes stacked fifty yards deep demanded attention. Perfectly easy.

I worked my way through the milling crowd towards the bike delivery. Hundreds of people had already arrived despite the early hour and the rain. The clouds above were thick and twisted, like a giant nebulous towel being wrung over yonder. Fortunately, above us directly it was only drizzling. It was delightful to this desert rat. Perfectly refreshing.

A surprisingly small tent was allocated for the organizing and distribution of all the shipped bikes. Several enthusiastic men and women waited with clipboards, ready to check off names and send the eager young men into the piles of boxes to muscle out specific parcels. Not seeing Aaron anywhere nearby, I went ahead with the process. Because the expo had only officially opened thirty minutes ago, there was no wait. Perfect timing.

Yes, it was all going as planned. After months of slaving and sweating, planning and stressing, it was all going to be as perfect as I had imagined.

A stranger approached. He was of average height but much bigger build. His huge shoulders and arms said bodybuilder, but his equally huge belly admitted those were days past. The man's dress and manner were rather slovenly, his face unshaven. All his hair was shot with grey, be it on his head, on his face, or protruding from his nose. A spandex biking jersey strained ludicrously over his paunch, the pattern of Vincent Van Gogh's *Starry Night* stretching stars into large, furry comets around a moon bloated to a white super giant. He seemed oddly intent on me.

He moved through the crowd, snarfing down a cheap microwave burrito. Under one armpit was the smashed wrapper of another. He finally made eye contact with me. His gaze was bold and handsome, intense beneath a strong brow. He quickly crammed the remains of the meal into his mouth—meaning the entire second half of the burrito—swallowing it in a painfully forced gulp. The stranger beamed at me and offered his hand. His vice-like grip made me squirm.

"I'm Cheek!" he said enthusiastically. "I'll be riding with you!"

Who the Hell was this?

CHAPTER THREE

Meet Cheek

RAGBRAI began in 1973 as a six-day ride across the state by a couple of newspaper columnists. The silly men envisioned a fun, if long, ride for just the two of them—or, at the most, maybe a few more Des Moines Register colleagues. Yet nearly 120 people made it across the state. The whole experience was so much fun they did it again the next year. Repeating the labor of love wasn't surprising, but the growth was: 2,000 riders showed up! Sweat, pork, and pie make a heady combination. Add beer and you've got a slice of Heaven. The tour grew so popular that it soon exceeded 10,000 riders. There it was capped, lest the small towns be utterly overwhelmed. Though volume no longer grew, variety certainly did, annually attracting riders from all fifty states and many nations. Thus, from the very beginning RAGBRAI existed entirely to welcome new riders and make new friends.

But *this* guy...?

"Who are you again?" I asked the thick, grizzled, yet strangely intense man.

"Cheek," he repeated simply, as if that was the most common name in the world.

Cheek paused to finish swallowing his burrito—a procedure I had assumed was complete since we were already talking. For a long moment he bobbed his neck up and down, up and down, not unlike a chicken swallowing a particularly long worm. Once satisfied, he resumed his explanation. "I was a last-minute add on. Aaron's my mate."

"Last minute," I repeated dubiously. "...for a *five hundred mile* bike ride."

"Yep," he said. "No sweat."

"Uh huh," I gave grudgingly. Though his excessive girth testified to his *not* being ready, it was a wonderful fact that all shapes and sizes rode RAGBRAI. Even so, I asked lightly, "So did you get much biking in?"

"Not so much," he said cheerily. His enthusiasm was not particularly catching. "Don't worry. I spent a lot of time on a stationary bike. Lots of miles."

So much for the perfect reunion I had expected. Still, there was a chance this Cheek wouldn't be so disruptive. He belched. I winced.

Maybe not.

The rain stopped, but the clouds didn't disperse. Their bulk pressed down upon us from above. Humidity grew thick and cloying, enveloping like honey. Cheek didn't say anything for a moment, nor did I. The moment stretched. Soon it became an awkward silence.

"Whoa," Cheek suddenly exclaimed, breaking the stalemate. "Look at that funky green bike!"

I turned around to see a mechanic pulling a bizarre, green-glowing bicycle from a tortured, rain-ruined box.

"I'll bet that set someone back," he commented. "The cables and even tires match."

The tall, aproned mechanic finished securing the glowing frame of the bike to his work stand. Nearby he set the two wheels, both with rim, spokes, tires, and even reflectors all in matching Day-Glo green. He just stared at it all, rubbing a dirty hand through a receding hairline. Finally he looked up and, as if he had just heard Cheek, replied, "I don't think so. This was spray painted."

"What kind of a weirdo would do that?" Cheek asked, approaching out of curiosity. "Look at that! Even the satchels are spray painted. Brake cables... everything. The gears look gunked up with it. Everything but the seat. Huh!"

"I already had enough issues with the seat," I muttered.

Cheek's mouth pursed for a moment, then suddenly split into a wide grin. "This is *yours*? Why'd you paint it?"

"Yes," bemoaned the mechanic, shaking his head at the gummed up gears. He looked like I had stolen his lunch money. "Why?"

"A moment of self-loathing," I said cryptically.

"At least the brakes rubbed a path clean on the rims," the mechanic commented. "Otherwise I wouldn't let you ride this tomorrow."

The man proceeded to assemble the bike in a whirl. Despite appearing older than Cheek's and my forty-ish years, he proved far more spritely than the both of us. He hopped this way and that, front and back, ratcheting ratchets and screwing screws. He mounted and spun the wheels, eyeing them expertly for wobbling, then adjusted brake strength and gear fluidity. At the very end, he finally addressed the sticking point I encountered when boxing the hateful thing. He pawed at the pedal for a bit, then frowned at its lack of proper response. Finally he said, "Righty tighty, lefty loosy."

"I know that!" I snapped. I apologized immediately. "I'm sorry. That thing really drove me nuts."

He merely smiled, unperturbed.

"Pedals are on opposite sides of the crank," he explained. "So they're reverse of each other. You were tightening it."

I took pains not to meet Cheek's amused gaze. It was too embarrassing to admit I had tried *both* directions unsuccessfully. Cheek snorted in amusement when the mechanic procured a wrench with a whopping yard-long handle. He wrested the pedal free, cleaned it, and reattached it properly.

"Done!" he said, unclamping the green bike from the work stand and setting it on the wet concrete. "I spent an extra fifteen minutes tweaking it."

"Did my Vegas guys do something wrong?"

"No, not wrong," he said generously, "Just not that good. I hope they didn't charge you much."

I snorted and handed him his shockingly small— or, rather, reasonable-in-the-normal-world—fee.

Cheek's bike came up next, just as a roar of thunder shocked the expo. It was so sudden and so loud we all jumped, surprised as any prey on the savannah. Lower grumbles followed, snarling over the tents.

"Uh oh," said the mechanic. "The bottom of your box is missing. Looks like it got wet from sitting in the rain and sheered off when they moved it. I hope everything's in there."

Cheek just watched. Things *were* missing. Lots of things. An absent cable was provided by the mechanic. The aero bars could not be mounted due to missing screws. Mechanic to the rescue again. What he couldn't fix was the front brake assembly. Missing were not a few screws, but the entire thing.

The mechanic rubbed his sweaty forehead again and pondered. Finally he regarded the heaps of foam padding and balled-up tape and admitted, "Doesn't look like we're gonna find it in this mess. I'd take pictures if I were you, so you can get reimbursement from the shipping company. To be honest, though, I don't think it fell out the bottom."

"Why not, sir?" Cheek asked.

"It's not standard to remove it for packing. Did you box it yourself, or the shop?"

"Shop."

"Yeah, well, there's probably a mechanic somewhere scratching his head trying to figure out where the extra front brake on his bench came from. Most of us are all gear and no brains."

"*That describes all men!*" shouted a woman passing by. She was hunched in the rain, but her jersey clearly read Team Rude Girl.

"Anyway, considering how dusty the bike is... well, to be honest, I could tell by the dust patterns that it hasn't had a front brake in months."

Cheek answered my questioning look with a shrug and a glib, "Stationary bike, remember?"

"Lots of miles," I agreed, quoted from earlier.

"High setting and everything," Cheek added with a twinkle in his eye.

A commotion in the rain called our attention outward. A trio of riders in jerseys hunched together, shoulders touching, trying unsuccessfully to shelter a single slice of pie. While three plastic forks jabbed, a passerby accosted them.

"Where's the pie?" he asked.

"You'll not get another one like this, my friend," came the gloating answer from a lady's apple-filled mouth. "We have the last piece!"

"Damn you!" he cried, shaking his fist in mock anger.

Only then did we notice that hundreds of riders dashed from tent to tent, or marched in small groups through crowded aisles between. Umbrellas were absent. Smiles were everywhere. The expo was on!

"Ten thousand riders," the mechanic commented in wonder. "That's half the size of my hometown!"

"Where are you from, sir?"

"I have a bike shop in Wisconsin," he said. "RAGBRAI hires out about a dozen small town bike shop owners every year. This is my second year. I'm still in awe."

"You like it, then?"

"I love it!" he beamed. "It's exhausting—fifteen hour days—but the profit makes up for it."

"As does the beer," Cheek observed.

"As does the pie," the mechanic clarified with a grin. "I'm on duty day and night. You know, fifteen thousand riders is the average amount of riders from a city of four hundred thousand. I think Glenwood here has, like, five thousand. Anyway, you'll need to find a front brake somewhere in the expo. There's ten shop tents, so someone'll have one. The whole thing's about to officially open."

"Good," I said, "'cause I need to get me one of *those*."

I pointed to the neighboring tent selling packaged bike seats. Specifically I pointed to a seat with a vicious-looking hole down the center that looked distressingly well-suited for a scrotum. Too horrified to even joke about such a thing, I instead changed anatomy, "Need a cigar-cutter mounted to your bike post? To cut off your butt..."

Nobody noticed my lame joke. That suited me fine—people usually only catch the bad ones! They were distracted by a magnificent sight in the rain.

There, piercing the mist and clouds above the tiny town of Glenwood, flew a Stealth Bomber! There was no mistaking the vehicle as it cut through patch after patch of rain-shredded clouds. Its approach was incredibly slow, giving it the Hollywood effect of being extra large, like some alien mother ship. It flew so low as to almost pass through the sports field's goal posts like a folded-paper football.

"Would you look at that!" I cried, stepping out from under the tent for a better view. I had never before seen a Stealth Bomber in flight, in person. Its flat black bat-wing design looked ultra sleek, ultra modern—and ultra wicked.

"That's a Northrop Grumman B-2 Spirit," Cheek said.

"Looks like a Stealth Bomber to me."

"That's what I said, my dear boy," he said lightly. "Looks like they're flying at the lowest legal limit. It only looks closer because a B-2's a lot bigger than you think."

The vehicle slowly spun about on its axis, performing a surprisingly casual barrel roll. It moved so slowly I wondered how it didn't fall from the sky. The playful maneuver earned a chorus of oohs and aahs from the crowd. I was shocked even more when the flying wing spun to reveal a profile thin as a playing card; a giant, flying ace of spades.

"Obviously from Offutt Air Force Base in Omaha," Cheek added, unimpressed by the aerial aerobics. "It's home to the 55th Wing. Air Force has a big recruiting team riding this year. Putting on a show for y'all."

After fully securing the entire crowd's attention, the Stealth Bomber suddenly shot off into the sky like a rocket. A moment later was felt, rather than heard, a deep BOOM. Windows rattled all across the school. Auto alarms yelped from afar. This action finally made an impression on Cheek—a bad one. His strong brow furrowed in obvious annoyance at such antics.

"How do you know so much?" I asked, stepping back under cover of the tent.

He shrugged dismissively and said, "I talked to the Air Force team 'cause I did the Navy team for three years."

"So are you a Navy pilot," I asked brightly, "like Maverick in *Top Gun*?"

"Do I look like Maverick in *Top Gun*?" Cheek deadpanned.

"Um... not exactly," I admitted uncomfortably, trying not to provoke his struggling spandex.

Cheek just smiled and said, "Quite right, my boy. Quite right."

"Navy's cool," I continued, trying to recover some dignity. "My father served four years in the Navy. I spent four years at sea myself, though working on cruise ships. What do you do in the Navy?"

"For twenty years I've been there," he said. "Retiring in three weeks. Can I just forget about it all for a bit?"

"Of course," I said. "Hey, you've earned it. I always forget to actually thank our service men and women, so let me express my appreciation for your work."

Cheek opened his mouth to say something, but then thought better of it. Instead he just stepped out into the rain.

"Historic flooding this summer has the Missouri River off limits to RAGBRAI bicyclists hoping to do the traditional back tire dip in the Muddy Mo to officially start their trek across the state of Iowa. Because of surface water flooding, mandatory evacuations have been ordered in western Mills County between Interstate 29 and the Missouri River. Roads and farmland west of Interstate 29 are inundated with surface water flooding and persons who enter the evacuated area and attempt to go to the Missouri River are subject to a citation and/or fine."

So squawked a radio blaring from the Chain Condom tent. Crotch lubes and chain condoms were *not* what I expected from my 'wholesome Midwest experience.' Throughout the tent were murmurs, rumors, and debates, raging through riders and vendors like a virus.

"No tire dip means no RAGBRAI!"

"I've dipped eight years running, and I'm not gonna stop now. I can swim."

"The Iowans won't let us down. They'll think of something."

While most riders preferred to debate the *real* issues before them, such as 'Beer!' vs. 'Pie!', the radio commenced with incidentals, such as the evacuation of nearby Hamburg.

"Half the town of Hamburg, Iowa was ordered to evacuate their homes within 24 hours after a levee broke. These floods are set to surpass the worst in the history of the state, including the damage done in 1993—ultimately costing over fifty lives and $15 billion in damages—and rival the 1952 devastation.

"The only time the Missouri River has been higher in the past six decades was in 1952. During that flood, the river crested above 44 feet at Sioux City, Iowa. This summer, the river has already reached as high as 37 feet at Sioux City. Precise comparisons between this year and 1952 are difficult because five major dams have been built since then and the Missouri River was also dredged to make it an additional 8 to 10 feet deeper. This means the volume of water has already surpassed that of 1952."

I was outwardly concerned for the welfare of the local people, but inwardly haunted by the ride ahead. I whined about riding in the rain. Didn't wet pavement get slippery? I was used to tires tackily gripping the road—'cause they were melting—and terrified that bikes could hydroplane across puddles.

After two hours of exploring and shopping and debating at the expo, Cheek found a front brake and got his bike up and running. And, best of all, we finally met up with Aaron.

Aaron was a big man in all ways. Tall, he had a big, wide nose and big, full lips for a big, habitual smile. He had big, bold ears escaping from curly hair. That was a lot of big to fit onto one head, and still didn't take into account the biggest thing of all: his brain. Oh, he also had a big waistline. While he may not have had the good fortune to look like Harrison Ford, that didn't stop him from acting like him. For what was ultimately biggest about the man were his ambitions. Aaron was a doer of diverse physical, intellectual, and spiritual activities. He dug archeological history in Israel, studied college abroad in England, and made the pilgrim trek to Machu Picchu. All this on top of brewing his own beer, bottling his own wine, and cooking his own culinary masterpieces.

Perhaps the most impressive characteristic of Aaron was how he had learned to overcome a stutter that had been so debilitating for him at school. No doubt he wouldn't care to be reminded of it, but oratory was something I focused upon heavily—in particular the sound of my own voice, which I apparently adored. Aaron's discovery of a solution was inspiring. Said solution was brilliant in its simplicity, too. Over the years he learned to anticipate the onset of a stutter and, instead of allowing it to drag out the beginning of a sentence interminably, he learned to repeat the first few words twice. Somehow this tricked that rascally part of his brain refusing to be concise. Now instead of appearing verbally handicapped, he just seemed eager.

After a warm hug, for we hadn't actually seen each other in a decade, Aaron shook hands with Cheek.

"You guys, you guys getting along?" Aaron asked.

"Sure," said Cheek, scratching his hip.

I just smiled and asked, "Where's Doc?"

"Dad's busy until dinner. The RV's set up and close to here, so we can drop off your stuff and head to town. Our phones aren't working too well, so we'll all meet at the square. It'll be crowded, but can't be that big."

"Dinner!" Cheek exclaimed. "I'm hungry."

Apparently he had already forgotten about the two burritos he ate just two hours ago. So to an early dinner we went. The central square of town was not very far away and, since the rain had stopped, we walked. We strode along sidewalks overflowing with people, gear, and bikes past the yards of houses overflowing with people, gear, and tents. The residents of Glenwood were proud to host the opening of RAGBRAI and had opened their properties accordingly. Though signs and banners sagged in rain-logged fatigue, porches and steps made up for it with homeowners waving enthusiastically. The feeling of welcome was palpable, the excitement electric.

Yet drama ensued.

A large bus rumbled by, catching our attention. Originally an old school bus, it had been customized for a RAGBRAI team. Across the entire roof was a huge metal platform bristling with bicycles, the front holding a rack of tires. The entire bus had been painted white and adorned with red flames, while over the windshield was painted in bold letters 'WRONG'. The back window was filled with painted flames and the warning, *"This is the wrong bus."* Below grinned mischievously the large faces of two devils.

As the bus drove by, arms waggled from out the

windows, with shouts and jeers erupting from inside. I imagined this having happened plenty when it was still a school bus, but such comparisons stopped when one bold man stuck his entire head out a window to shout at us, "I screwed your mother, you bastards!"

"I've seen a surprising number of teams recycling old school busses," Aaron commented. Then he added with a snigger, "Well, not as surprising as *that* one. Talk about wrong!"

I shared his laugh, but Cheek saw things differently. He was furious. His face clouded darker than the sky above and he ran in pursuit. Aaron was shocked at Cheek's behavior, whereas I was more surprised at his explosive speed. Sluggish he may have appeared, but that man could move!

"I'll take you *all* on, damn it!" Cheek shouted at the departing bus, shaking a fist into the air. Despite his impressive speed, however, he had no hope of catching up to the bus. He slowed to a trot, then grudgingly stopped. When we caught up to him, Aaron pointed out, "They were, they were just joking."

"My mother is off limits," Cheek grumbled.

"*Everybody's* mother is off limits," Aaron said. "That was the point, I think. They were intentionally doing 'wrong' things."

Team names were clever enough to make an ad writer green with envy. Take the Cranky Bastards, for example: their logo was an adorable, frowning personified bike crank. Then there was Team Pour Decisions with a picture of empty cocktail glasses. Strange to see those on child riders. While all team names were clever, most involved puns, such as our own Tire Dips. Aaron was particularly drawn to Team Cuisine: *'Eating up the miles!'*

Other team names were delightfully naughty. For example, there was the Bike-Sexuals, a team of predominantly young men and women who had been *'Coming Out of the Closet Since 2010.'* The naughtiness was implied by the words *'Getting Off'* on their shorts—a warning they were dismounting their bikes, no doubt. My personal favorite was Team Camo-toe, a group of attractive women wearing exceptionally tight camouflage spandex. We all smiled at an adorable elderly couple staring at them, trying to understand the joke. We agreed that if they didn't know it already, we weren't about to enlighten them. Also potentially naughty was Team Lube It: *'You Buy It, We Apply It.'*

"If you wanna know what RAGBRAI is all about," Cheek offered, indicating a T-shirt before us.

RAGBRAI for Dummies:
1. Drink beer
2. Apply Butt Cream
3. Drink Beer
4. Watch Out for Rumbles
5. Drink Beer
6. Take a Nap
7. Drink Beer
8. Stop at Beekman's
9. Drink Beer
10. Dip Your Tires

Aaron eventually commented, "I'm excited to see Team Roadkill."

"In action?" I asked dubiously.

"It's not, it's not what you think," Aaron responded with a smile. "Whenever they pass anything dead on the road they claim it as their own. I don't know how. I'm curious."

"Back home, they'd claim it by cookin' it," Cheek grunted. Seeing the reaction this statement evoked in Aaron—the consummate chef—Cheek quickly explained, "I'm from rural Virginia, remember? 'Sides, it's not as nuts as some of the stuff you weirdos eat in hoity-toity liberal Portland. Really, Aaron, cryogenic foods?"

Aaron surrendered with a laugh, but I was too intrigued to let it end there.

"Do tell," I ribbed Aaron.

"Allow me," Cheek interrupted. "'Cryogenic food pairing is the art of perfectly combining two normally incompatible foods that have similar molecular components, thus forming blends of original flavors beyond the pale of nature.' But really, Aaron... fusion of oyster and kiwi? That's Team Wrong for you."

I stopped and stared at Cheek, awed by his recital. Seeing my expression, Aaron mused, "Didn't I tell you that Cheek's full of surprises?"

"You didn't tell me about him at all," I muttered under my breath.

In the packed square, leaning against a sign that boldly proclaimed 'NO WHEELED VEHICLES'—upon which also leaned no less than half a dozen bikes—was

Aaron's father. That he would gravitate to such a spot was not surprising, for Doc had a well-honed sense of irony. A hale and hearty mid-sixties man, Doc looked every bit Aaron's father, without the genetically moderating influence of Aaron's mom, of course. The only real difference in appearance between father and son was that Doc shaved his head. In behavior they were much the same as well, though even Aaron agreed that Doc was far and away the 'biggest' of us all.

We four enjoyed a simple meal in Glenwood but had to cut it short when the community tornado sirens went off. Doc leapt up immediately, fearing the RV's awning would be damaged in the gusts that topped 40 mph. I somehow managed to refrain from scoffing aloud that I had been riding into 40 mph winds for months now—a rare but long overdue moment of self-censorship. Of course, Nevada winds were different, being strengthened by their cascade down mountains and focused through passes. In Iowa, winds were not feared for their 'pushing' strength as much as how they reacted with other wind currents higher in the atmosphere. Yes, my first day back in Iowa and Tornado Alley kicked in! No doubt this was why they filmed parts of the movie *Twister* here. This did not bode well for the week.

After securing the awning it was time to assemble my tent. Aaron, his father, and Cheek were dwelling in the RV, so they were already set up. There was room for me, too, but I wanted a taste of the real RAGBRAI. For thousands of riders, that meant tents. Not everybody, though. Beside us rumbled up a huge semi labeled *'Big Bob's Sleeping'*. Big Bob towed a full-sized semi trailer with a series of doors down its length, each complete with folding steps. Behind each door was six bunks, the last allocated for showers. Some camping!

I assembled my tent between the wheeled mammoths on a slope, being the only patch of grass available. The rainfly was a mighty struggle, for in two years of using the tent I had never before attached it— another dubious perk of living in Las Vegas.

Sleeping in the tent promised several challenges. First was the rather severe angle, for the synthetic sleeping bag gleefully slid across the synthetic flooring. Second was the little issue of heat. Iowa in late July was extremely muggy. I had not been particularly grateful of Doc's announcement that the night was to have a heat index of 120°, calculated by adding the temperature and humidity together. I may complain of Vegas heat, but at least I slept in air conditioning. But my biggest concern was rain. Rainfly or no, if the downpour recommenced I imagined myself sliding— tent and all—right down into the street. The sodden ground had all but spat out my stakes with disdain.

Once set up, we stayed put. Perhaps it was due to Aaron, or rather his only previous experience with RAGBRAI revelry.

"Back in '93," Aaron narrated, "I was lifeguarding in Decorah as a skinny 20-year-old college student. On the busiest day of summer we might have five hundred people a day, including kids attending swim lessons. The day RAGBRAI rolled through we had at least *ten times* that. I remember it well, partly because it was my first eighteen-hour shift—all-nighters for class excepted, of course.

"It started slowly, when a few tents appeared in the adjacent fields, then more on the lawns across the street. Then cyclists came through the turnstile and never stopped coming. They used our showers, hopped in the pool, flirted with the lady guards, ignored our frantic whistling, and—most shocking of all—ate *all* of our bad concession ice cream. Cyclists introduced themselves from all over the world, including Japan, Germany and the Republic of Ireland. I'll never forget how that quiet, foggy morning with deer in the adjacent fields morphed into a rowdy pool with so many drunk cyclists that we literally couldn't see the surface of the water. It was sheer mayhem. By the end of the night we were left with three inches of mud in the locker room and overflowing tills. Around midnight we forced out the stragglers and staggered home."

"Sounds amazing," I commented.

"What was, what was amazing was what happened on the way home!" Aaron added with a laugh. "In the interest of time I cut through some woods and in the darkness felt a rock in my Birkenstocks. Too tired to stop I kept going and collapsed into bed. It was only the next morning that I discovered it wasn't a rock in my sandals, but a poor frog that had somehow hopped under my sole and gotten smeared across the footbed. I knew exactly how it felt. True story."

"As if anybody would make *that* up," I reassured

him.

Thus with Aaron's story—and perhaps our advancing age—we were content to lay low. That is not to say there were no regrets. The expo offered something for everyone, including countless musicians cranking out everything from Southern gospel to golden oldies. Of particular horror to me, however, was an act called *'Elvis and Marilyn, Together at Last.'* I couldn't escape Elvis to save my life. I was still scarred by having worked on the Las Vegas Strip by the stage for Big Elvis, the world's fattest Elvis impersonator. To be fair, despite his 400-plus pounds he was actually quite expressive, though only in comparison to his previous years and moniker of Fat Elvis, when he weighed in at a whopping 950. Alas, we also missed out on the expo's World Tire Changing Championship, which tried to topple the record of just over one minute. For me it was closer to fifteen, if I figured it out at all.

No doubt that first night we were hobbled by a bit of ethnocentrism regarding entertainment—certainly I was—and more than a little trepidation at beginning such a physical challenge hungover. Still, Doc cracked open a bottle of whiskey, so we had our libations. I had a cigar and offered them around, but Aaron abstained until after the tour. Cheek, perhaps not surprisingly, sucked down two stogies and guzzled large amounts of booze. As midnight neared Cheek boldly thrust himself up to his feet. Grabbing two large handfuls of belly fat and giving them a jiggle, he proclaimed for all, "I will lose *all this* by the end of RAGBRAI." It was most inspiring.

Our little group began dispersing for the night. At the end I was left with Doc for a few minutes, which gave me an opportunity to ask something that had been on my mind.

"So Doc," I began. "You're like, a high-level specialist radiologist who is semi-retired. You've made a fortune with your uncanny ability to analyze and interpret X-ray images of soft tissues, right? So if I break my leg or something... well, when was the last time you fixed anything like that?"

"If it's a broken leg, I'll fix you up no problem," Doc said reassuringly. Then he paused to peer into the remainder of his rye. Finally he added, "But if you have an ingrown toenail, I am sorry to say, you are screwed. I simply don't remember how to fix that one."

With that he rose and retired to the RV.

Sleep was minimal, as the party refused to end. RAGBRAI had gone through a long, nearly self-destructing party phase. The riders became so wild that towns began refusing to host them. With such an undeniable economic boom from tens of thousands of visitors, that was astonishing. Realizing the danger to the touring tradition, the organization cracked down. Now RAGBRAI boasted those days were over. One aspect of their success was emphasis on team participation, almost to the point of denying individuals, for a team was inherently self-policing. But when I heard sirens through the thin walls of my tent, I began to wonder if anything had really changed.

At 6AM sharp I was awakened by an old-fashioned triangle bell. Someone rang it madly, conjuring images of the Old West days. I expected at any moment to hear a cry of 'come and get it!' The bell was even loud enough to penetrate the RV.

"Who the Hell, who the Hell is doing that?" a voice groaned through the window.

Cheek's groggy response answered, "Team Wrong."

It was 7AM. I was in a line of thousands of people. It was already over 90°, 80% humidity. Heat index forecast 110°. I was waiting to dip my bike in a tub of muddy water. It was teeming with catfish. I was in spandex.

People ribbed me over my bike. "Yeah, yeah," I said lackadaisically, too tired and sweaty to bother explaining for the 200th time why I spray painted my bike Day-Glo green.

"Dad said this morning floods are much worse than the last recorded high," Aaron said, squinting at the mist-dripping woods as if he could penetrate them to see the swollen river beyond. "Thanks to the rain yesterday. The Army Corps of Engineers reports that runoff on the river is the largest since record keeping began in 1898. Can you believe that? That's all, that's all despite dredging the river *ten feet deeper*."

"Mmph," Cheek agreed sleepily.

But where there's a will, there's a way. Members of the Glenwood boys high school and middle school cross country teams had gathered a tank containing water from the Missouri River. The tank was located near the softball complex. They even caught the live catfish. Gotta have the catfish.

An onlooker commented in wonder, "I can't believe in the midst of all of the flooding and their own problems the wonderful folks in Iowa are concerned about us dipping our tires!"

Another observed, "This is one of the reasons I love this state so much. Nothing beats the people of Iowa!"

"Hear hear!" I called out, which Aaron eagerly seconded.

"Mmph," Cheek agreed sleepily.

Yet I was nervous. Not about the ride. Not even about getting stung by a catfish. I was nervous at seeing all these people I would have to engage, navigate, avoid. I had trained on lonely stretches of desert highway. The only time I ever rode with people I was nearly hurled off the road into a gulch. If a falling Tour de France rider could take out a dozen others, how would these thousands of non-professionals fare? How would I fare? It was a terrifying prospect.

But the energy of the tire dip was all positive. It was palpable. There were no grumblings about the undue length of time required, or how cumbersome it all was. We were embracing the ritual despite some pretty hefty odds. Overcoming the worst flood in the Midwest's recorded history was nothing to sneeze at. We could do anything—we were ready!

"Remember how I said I trained lots of miles on the stationary bike?" Cheek piped up suddenly.

A rustle of spandex as both Aaron and I turned to

regard him.

"Yeah... not so much."

The moment came. A small ramp led up to a surprisingly small tank of river water. In fact, it was just a plastic blue kiddie-pool! With catfish. We Tire Dips swung our bikes in awkward unison to wet the rear tires. Tire dipping ritual... *begun!* At that glorious moment, 500 miles seemed insignificant. We were gonna close that ritual by dipping our front tires in the Mississippi, come Hell or high water—both being very likely.

We rushed down the platform, across the trampled, soaked grass, to merge with the line of cyclists, many of whom chose to skip the ceremony and hit the road fast. Hit the road is what we did, too! So much excitement and buildup, a year of tension, training and preparation, all for this glorious first day. Yes, we were surging into a dream! Cheek—suddenly very much alive—launched uphill, powering past everyone and bellowing the whole way. Within moments he was lost to sight in the long throng of bikers.

"I sense he'll be panting and wheezing over the next hill," I commented.

"Adrenaline does wonders," Aaron agreed.

Up the hill we surged, too. We were doing it: we were embarking on a perfect adventure with each other. We were going to wrest that birthright of every Iowan, that dream of excellence—wrest it I say!—and place it above our mantel or mental trophy shelf of personal triumphs.

Or not.

Sixty seconds later everything came to a screeching halt.

CHAPTER FOUR

Tire Dips

"Green machine is down!"

Up and away from the rapidly dismantling expo the road rose, seductively hugging the curves of a hill crammed with green leafy trees. The pavement beneath the canopy was yet clammy with night's wet. This was the perfect road to begin a mammoth journey: natural beauty beckoned, as did just enough challenge to spike enthusiasm from the get-go. All riders felt one with adventure, all smiled and joked even as they panted and sweat—all, but for two.

"Bad start, not-so-Jolly Green Giant."

The barbs were tossed lightly. Help was within sight, after all—right next to thousands of adults waiting to play in a kiddie pool—so nobody worried about a breakdown on this early leg of the ride. But it wasn't even a leg yet, or even an ankle. We had barely gotten to a toe!

"Don't make him angry—you wouldn't like him when he's angry!"

Despite good intentions, the amiable ribbing annoyed me. For it wasn't my attention-grabbing green bike that had broken down. It was Aaron's.

Aaron was riding a time-tested, reliable 2003 Marin Mill Valley. Though a black-framed mountain bike with straight handlebars, he had adapted it to a city bike. For two years he rode it around Monterey and Pebble Beach, until retiring it to storage. RAGBRAI prompted a retrieval and dusting, a fresh lube and new road tires. In short, his bicycle was pedigreed, tried and true—it totally sucking within 200 yards notwithstanding.

"I've never, I've never had a single flat in a thousand miles," Aaron said, amused by the hobbling timing of a mechanical problem. "Or any other issue except when I bent the middle chain ring. But that was due to my monster legs."

But it wasn't a flat. His joviality died a quick, slashing death. He frowned down at the troubled rear wheel, oddly contorted over bent spokes. Other spokes, broken entirely, jabbed outward to spike human ankles more eagerly than catfish in a tire dip. Aaron's right ankle dribbled blood from where the exploding metal got him.

"The derailer," he identified in shock. "It's been pushed in so the spokes would hit it. This rim is completely wasted!"

"So the mechanic reassembled it wrong?"

Aaron shook his head, fighting anger as the realization of a serious issue took root. He groused, "Can you believe I rode this a full thirty minutes yesterday to make sure all was well? I don't know how this is even possible. It's been safe on the bike rack all night. I'd laugh if I wasn't so mad."

He certainly didn't look very mad. Aaron handled the situation well, though I sensed it was absolutely infuriating him. Outwardly he only released a sedate, if repeating, "I'm so mad... I'm so mad."

"Couldn't you have just been stung by a catfish or something?" I said, frowning at the blood soaking into his sock. I was trying to lighten the mood—a refreshing rarity, for usually I was the one grumbling.

"Would have been preferable," Aaron agreed. "I hope not all the mechanics have packed up and moved further afield yet. At least the expo is nearby."

"Shockingly, *embarrassingly* nearby," I clarified.

"I can't use the sag wagon yet," Aaron moaned. "Isabel bet me I wouldn't make it. My wife is nothing if not supportive. Even if I do ultimately fail, I can't do it in the first *two hundred yards!*"

"Well, let's settle on a plan," I said. "Let's call Cheek and tell him, and get you to the mechanic. We got a long day ahead of us."

Aaron pulled out his cell phone, but immediately pocketed it with a rigid face. "Nothing. I haven't had reception since we got here. I think the cell towers are overloaded. There's fifteen thousand people using towers designed for probably two or three."

"I hadn't thought of that. Good thing my phone

broke before the ride, or I would find that frustrating."

Aaron chuckled and said, "Breakdown within seconds, no way to contact Dad, no way to contact Cheek, no idea where the camp will be and no way to communicate it to us. No sag wagon coming. It's already hot as Hell. This is like *The Comedy of Errors!*"

"Don't forget you're bleeding," I added helpfully. "That's good, though. All manly adventures require bleeding."

Eventually Aaron ordered me to go ahead with the ride and he would walk back down to the remnants of the expo. If he couldn't find a mechanic or a shuttle to one, he would find a land line to call Doc, who was probably outside the cell dead zone that followed the bulk of riders. I wanted to stay with him, but Aaron was adamant. It was so horrendously disheartening to fail within seconds of starting, he insisted on minimizing its impact on me.

"I'll catch up," he said. "I can't bear the thought of my mechanical issue ruining your joy of the ride."

"Joy of the ride," I repeated with a snort. "Yeah, right. At least Cheek's nowhere to be found."

I immediately regretted the last statement. Cheek was Aaron's friend, and my antagonizing was completely selfish. Fortunately Aaron was unfazed, replying, "He grows on you. You'll see."

I wasn't so sure, but had oodles of respect for Aaron's opinion. I resolved to check my opinion of Cheek until the end of the first day. A man should be judged by his actions, not his appearance—and certainly not by his presence!

Despite our setback and grumblings, I was actually in fine spirits. We were here and on the road to adventure. Well, on the *side* of the road to adventure, but that was just temporary. The excitement of nearby thousands was most contagious. Perhaps, just perhaps, it could cut through my Vegas disdain. Maybe, just maybe, I could become less of a sourpuss. Was it even possible? No doubt Aurelia would say, "Ain't no way with muh beeotch."

A couple miles down the road I met up with Cheek. He was waiting at the roadside near the freshly-mown ditch of a large farmhouse that had opened its lands to vendors. Cheek was easy to spot due to his large belly and distinctive chamois. The spandex shorts featured letters spelling 'NAVY' that were as faded and distended as the man who bore them. Fingerless gloves unconsciously fidgeted to fists.

"Pancakes!" Cheek said impatiently when I pulled up.

"Nice to see you, too," I said. Before I had even hopped off my bike he was already marching up to the barn. The man was incorrigible. His breakfast, merely one hour and one breakdown ago, had been two jumbo muffins, a banana, and a big cookie.

I left my bike in the ditch beside Cheek's and a long, mixed jumble of others. Up the gravel driveway we went, passing a mottled snake of men and women in vibrant jerseys wiggling towards a trailer for coffee. Further up the sloping drive stood a much thicker and less restless mass of riders, waiting to enter a huge barn for heavier goods. The fresh morning air was tinged with the scent of large animals. We joined the line, I explained Aaron's breakdown, and asked Cheek to try calling him.

"Oops," Cheek responded. "Forgot to charge my phone."

"Oh, don't trouble yourself," I said, only half-joking. "Aaron's only bleeding and stuff."

"Bah!" Cheek scoffed. "Bleeding's good for the soul."

At least we concurred on that point, though I had little desire to admit it.

Cheek enjoyed his pancakes—extra butter, extra syrup—while I sipped coffee. We waited by the roadside in silence. Well, not total silence. His formidable teeth clicked loudly on the plastic fork, threatening to bite right through. Unable to stomach watching the ingestion of a carb-sugar-butter bomb, I instead scanned the throng of riders for Aaron's tell-tale jersey. It was bright yellow and decorated with images of evergreens and mountains. On every conceivable place for text, including the back, shoulders, and even under the armpits, was proudly written 'OREGON'. This was most fortunate, for identifying a particular rider among the thousands was no easy task. After a while, however, we agreed it was time to move on and somehow meet Aaron later.

"Pancakes good?" I asked, hiding a smile at Cheek's pawing of spilled syrup on his protruding jersey.

"Awesome! The thing I love about this trip is that I can get rid of *this*," he said, grabbing his belly. "This'll all be gone by the end of the week!"

"By eating pancakes?"

"Fuel, my dear boy. Fuel."

Lending action to his words, Cheek mounted his bike and immediately powered up the next hill with crazy emphasis—or, rather, recklessness. He left me in the dust, and I let him. I wondered if he knew how obvious it was that he couldn't use his bike's aero-bars because his huge belly prevented leaning far enough forward. I biked alone for a while and, surprisingly, found Aaron waiting further up the road.

"How...?"

"They had, they had me fixed in a jiffy," Aaron explained. "They didn't have to replace the rim, but only the broken spokes. The bent ones straightened when all the spokes were put into place. Five minutes and thirty bucks. I scored. Anyway, I thought you guys would be far ahead of me."

"Pancake stop," I explained. "Cheek took off like a bat out of Hell again. I'm surprised you didn't see him pass."

"Green machine's easy to spot in the crowd," Aaron observed. "I guess I missed Cheek. I only stopped to catch a breather after, well... after getting my ass kicked by a 50-year-old, one-legged lady."

"I beg your pardon?"

"It's simply awesome she's out here doing it," he quickly defended. Then he admitted with a chuckle, "but that doesn't mean I want to come in second."

Pride is a tricky thing. So, too, is expectation. The disastrous starting minutes notwithstanding, the first morning of RAGBRAI began looking like what I had expected. Side by side with Aaron, we rode through a serene, lovely land of knotty hills, short but steep, with many a copse of robust trees between them. Hillside flanks not hosting rows of ten-foot cornstalks exploded with wild grasses and wildflowers of immense variety and color.

I would have given almost anything to see those hills two hundred years ago, before man hacked down the head-high wild grasses, before man forged steel plows strong enough to cut topsoil pounded solid by trampling herds of buffalo numbering in the *millions*. The bounty of millennia of nature unobstructed seemed incomprehensible—almost as incomprehensible as man conquering it all in only a few decades. But I did not dwell on such thoughts, for islands of biodiversity survived everywhere; in hollows bristling with ancient trees, on hills flowing with waves of mixed grasses, along riverbeds teeming with life. These quiet acres of Western Iowa were lovely as anything I'd seen in my fifty nations of traveling. Aaron concurred. Cameras clicked from passing riders, too.

We rounded a tree-lined curve, the road dropped, and suddenly we were assaulted by a huge billboard showing a photograph of a giant fetus on a plate. The caption read in bold, accusatory letters, *'WHY DID YOU KILL ME, MOMMY?'*

So much for serenity.

As if that were not jarring enough, Aaron rode directly into the next road hazard. From up ahead we heard cries of "Rumble!", but thought little enough of it. The road curved around yet another hill, then suddenly dropped more steeply than ever. A sudden, tight T-intersection loomed before us, with rumble strips added just to make it more lethal. I swerved into the oncoming lane to avoid the rumbles, but Aaron plowed right into them. The grooves jounced his entire bike like popcorn popping and his body convulsed as if electrocuted. The experience was so violent he nearly pitched into the embankment.

Screeching to a halt at the intersection, I asked him, "Are you OK?"

"I did that intentionally," he admitted, tonguing the inside of his cheek with a grimace. "I thought all the other cyclists were just being wimps, so I braved them. I won't do *that* again—I bit my cheek!"

The hills grew demanding. They were not particularly long, but intensely steep. Up, up we labored, only to careen downward fifty feet before laboring upward again. A line of cyclists, clustered in pairs or trios riding abreast, stretched as far as the eye could see forward and backward. The line wavered and swelled as small clusters split to pass others, fanned out then collapsed back in line. It was all surprisingly quiet.

My expectation of being lost in a chaotic crowd was happily proven wrong, in good part due to those hills. While undulations of the land kept getting higher, so did the temperature. Soon Aaron's expectations were fulfilled—and exceeded.

"I knew it would be hot," he said, wiping sweat from his brow for the umpteenth time. "Our hottest day this year was a rainy sixty-five degrees. I've got to slow down. I'm sorry."

"Don't be," I said pleasantly. "We knew these first two days would be tough."

"I was mentally prepared for ten thousand feet of elevation gain in two days," Aaron huffed, "but this heat is brutal. It's gotta be pushing a hundred already. Really, go on ahead. I'll meet you in the first town."

Once again, Aaron was being kind. I sensed this was less about his pride than worry over 'ruining' a friend's ride. Though all I wanted was to hang back with him, the polite response seemed to be to comply with his wishes. Alas, would I ever get a chance to spend quality time with Aaron? That was the only reason I was doing this!

If Aaron remained frustratingly absent, Cheek was maddeningly present. He waited at every single stop, which meant nearly every single farm house. After the pancakes, at the next farm he stopped for a muffin. The third was a slice of pie. After ensuring I saw him, he always powered on ahead and out of sight. This pattern continued until the first town of Silver City.

Silver City, Iowa boasted barely over one hundred houses. That level of dinkiness was hard to really believe—until I passed a brick town hall the size of a one-stall garage. Upon this stalwart implement of civil organization leaned Cheek.

"Beer!" he boomed as I neared. "They have an American Legion tent!"

"I'd really rather not," I protested mildly. "It's only 10AM and we have another fifty miles to ride."

"But the hills are starting to get steep and it's getting hot," he spluttered.

"Once the sweat starts I become a purist," I explained. "I'm in 'warrior mode'."

He chided with a snort, "Don't get cocky."

"That ship has sailed," I admitted.

Cheek continued with a bit of a whimper and said, "But, but, this is what you *do* at RAGBRAI. No *proeliator modus* here."

Staring at him incredulously, I asked, "Did you just speak to me in Latin? Now who sounds arrogant?"

"'Warrior mode'," he explained. "It doesn't belong here. This is my fourth RAGBRAI, so I would know."

"Fourth?" I asked, shocked. He mentioned he'd ridden on the Navy team, but never said three times! Cheek sure was quiet about certain things. "All right, I'll join you, but I won't drink."

Cheek waddled excitedly through some bales of hay that demarcated the entrance to the American Legion area. It was a green oasis of cool shade and soft grass. Music from a distant band sounded tinny through the humidity. I sat beneath a tree on some hay bales beside two women happily labeled Naughty Nightingales. Their white, nurse-like jerseys offered the picture of a sexy nurse and read, *'Feel Safe at Night: Sleep With a Nurse!'* Taped onto their helmets was the traditional nurse's cap, white with a red cross.

"Which branch?" a young woman asked me. She had a wide smile, sweat-streaked sunglasses, and a damp red handkerchief tying back her hair.

"Navy, ma'am!" Cheek answered for me, approaching with two plastic cups of foamy beer. He handed me one even as he chugged the other. It kind of grossed me out.

"There's a Navy team this year?" she asked. "I only saw the Air Force. They have like a hundred. I don't know how they'll keep them all in line."

"No joke," Cheek agreed. "Three years I did the Navy team. Couldn't party like we wanted, but it was kind of a paid vacation, you know? But I'm on leave this time."

"I was thin then," he added quickly, before finishing his beer with a loud smack of relief. He plucked the beer out of my hand and his chicken-with-a-worm necking resumed.

We chatted awhile with a feisty grey-haired Naughty Nightingale with some great stories. After securing a beer for the road, Cheek joined me in wandering back to the main banner aloft over the road. It was secured by two rented cranes, easily the tallest man-made constructs in Silver City. A live band entertained riders in an outdoor beer garden. At one point the Fire Chief took the microphone to thank the riders of RAGBRAI, saying revenues earned would finally allow the volunteer fire department to pave the rear bays of the fire station. After hearing that, I bought another beer. Cheek happily drank it.

Riders spontaneously joined in activities as

varied as their own shapes, sizes, and colors. One skinny lady led a group in performing handstands. Middle-aged bodies tumbled into the soft grass with childlike glee, earning grins aplenty from both observers and participants. Everybody loved everybody. I imagined this as some sort of little Woodstock, filled with enthusiastic sharing of music and love. And, of course, everyone was high. But in this case, high on life and discovery. I was a slow learner, though, finding little joy in the discovery of Cheek. Maybe I'd like him better if he tried a handstand. Instead I watched him chug another beer.

Not having found Aaron in the crowd, we rode anew. Cheek once again disappeared in a blaze of power. I pedaled onward alone, yet didn't feel that way. Chatting with the Naughty Nightingales and others in Silver City had provided a stark break from what I was used to; that is, big city ego-maniacs with no time to talk to even their neighbors. I was all too well aware of having become the same and relished the opportunity to talk to others. As we say in Iowa, 'there are no strangers, just friends you haven't met yet.' RAGBRAI appeared to be the ultimate expression of this credo.

The high point of the day's ride—that is, highest elevation—was identified by a sign that read, *'Congratulations! It's all downhill from here!'*. Of course, it was placed at the bottom of the hill. While such irony may not have been knee-slapping-guffaw-worthy, the cumulative groans it prompted became so.

Ultimately, Aaron, Cheek, and I went back and

forth for the next forty miles, together at times, splitting at others. This was mostly due to the damnable hills.

The Loess Hills (pronounced 'less') formed something of a 'western range' for Iowa along the Missouri River. These were created by the glaciers of the last ice age. Rather devilishly, they enjoyed grinding any earth they covered into a fine powder. This, I presumed, was vastly entertaining. Eventually they tired of pushing their weight around and retreated north, callously leaving behind vast mud flats topped with a fine-grained silt. Then it was the wind's turn to push everybody around, and it did just that. Eventually the silt was blown into dunes. Not just little mounds of dust, but big, nasty dunes hundreds of feet tall. When this dried up it was quite tough, but also highly unstable when wet. So then came water's turn to have its heyday. Over the millennia rain and rivers created sharp, extreme bluffs. Still not impressed? There is only one comparable spot on Earth, and that is as far away as Shaanxi, China.

Almost every farm participated in one manner or another, heat or no. Huge front yards, actually acres of freshly-mown hills leading to old farm houses, teemed with thousands of cyclists. Every shady tree protected a panting, sweating, but in no way defeated, rider. Many retired locals lounged in folding chairs, by the road if shade allowed, and talked with people pulling off. Dogs yipped about excitedly. Rather than being aggressive and barking or threatening strangers, they, too, felt the vibe of openness and curiosity, of connection. Too many new friends to wag your tail at!

I was simply delighted at seeing a large, aging farmer in overalls taking the day off to fill water bottles from his garden hose. Delighted by each and every rider, he asked where they were from and heartily welcomed them to Iowa.

One of my favorite things was seeing the bizarre and utterly unique methods people designed to provide water for the throng of thirsty riders. One farmer's contraption was a long hose bristling with nozzles every few feet. This was mounted atop two tall poles placed some fifty feet apart. Near the poles, taller riders on their tip-toes reached up to fill their bottles, leaving the sagging center for petite riders and children. Others were fire hydrants wearing strings of Mardi Gras beads, additional pipes fitted with levers for rapid filling. It was not unusual to see riders bent over to douse their heads... sometimes helmet and all.

Creativity was not reserved for watering devices, however. All manner of bike racks tickled the imagination. While most riders dropped their bikes in ditches and grass, others took advantage of whatever contraption someone took the time, thought, and effort to provide. Most common were monstrous tractors and combines playing tug of war with metal cables, stretching them taut about three feet off the ground. Easily a hundred bikes or more could be hooked on.

Perhaps the most surprising creativity of all, however, were jibes regarding the color of my bike. It took me a moment to recognize I was being hailed when someone shouted, "Hey, Mask!" Most common were 'leprechaun' and 'John Deere'. One rider, retired from a John Deere factory, took my bike as an opening. He rode alongside me, exhaustively narrating a story about pretty much every single tractor he built over his thirty-five-year career. He was so sweet I didn't have it in me to stop him, though by mile three I was praying for rescue. Even Cheek would have been welcome.

I then heard the strangest sound while laboring up a hill. Above the panting and groaning of a thickly bunched mass of riders rose a rough, grating cry. The sound began indistinct due to distance, then swelled to awful proportions. The wail rose to a fever-high pitch.

"CHAAAAHHHHPPP!!"

A high-speed police pursuit? An ambulance? I suffered a flash of panic, fearing the thick herd of riders would turn to stampede and I would be crushed. While frantically searching above the helmets of riders, I spied Cheek peddling calmly up ahead. I caught up and asked if he saw the ambulance.

"No ambulance," he replied. "Wasn't a siren."

"Then what was it?"

"You'll see later," he said knowingly.

Nobody else seemed concerned, so I dropped the issue. After a moment, Cheek gave me a disgusted look and said with annoyance, "Don't you sweat? It's over a hundred degrees."

"I live on the sun," I reminded him. "My wife sets the air conditioner at 90."

"That's crazy!"

"Still thirty degrees cooler than outside," I pointed out.

But heat was indeed becoming a serious issue. The heat index was topping 115°.

Biking up 4,300 feet of elevation over sixty miles was not easy, and at 90% humidity the air was unbearably muggy. Panting up the hills was hard enough without the added burden of breathing water. Riders dropped left and right. Each farm house sheltered more and more riders passed out in the shade. The sag wagon was working overtime, and not because of mechanical issues. People literally fainted from heat and dehydration. Most who were particularly susceptible, such as the aged—of which there were many—were taking extreme care and resting throughout the hot midday hours.

The route coasted down to the Nishnabotna River at the second host city, Carson. A local welding company had created a spinning Ferris wheel out of six bicycles—one for each town on the day's route. While it was a far cry from Cirque du Soleil, I found it perhaps more satisfying to view. There was great pride in Carson, particularly regarding their strawberry-rhubarb and apple pies. Carson and tiny Silver City, though places I could never possibly imagine living in, were truly charming. I adored their excitement at showing off to guests, even as they savvily took advantage of the inflow to build up or renovate. Carson's profits from selling a wide variety of foods and pie were destined to build a planned Carson Community Park and renovate the Dreamland Theatre downtown. In short, it was a place worthy of buying lunch.

We met up with Aaron in Carson. His face was puffy and pink from the heat, so we took a long rest in the shade of an impressive old brick bank building. Aaron and Cheek bought some grilled sweet corn, while I had a sandwich wrap with locally-produced bacon in honor of my wife. Once ready for the next push, Aaron and I gratefully bought frozen water bottles from the local Girl Scouts to put in our bikes' water bottle cages, while Cheek filled his CamelBak with ice. This time when we started off together, Cheek did not power on ahead. He made noises that he wanted to remain with Aaron for awhile, but I knew better. The heat was clearly debilitating both my companions. We had to stop again for a cooling break within mere miles, but couldn't have chosen a better place to do so.

The Canoyer Country Greenhouse was a sprawling structure in a scattered line of new homes along the old highway. Here, nestled among copious flowering plants and beside bubbling fountains, were numerous food vendors. Tom's Turkey, a RAGBRAI favorite, offered marinated turkey fillet sandwiches or smoked turkey legs for those on the go. Pastafari was the popular healthy option, featuring pasta with garden vegetables and fresh pesto. For those who'd had enough punishment and just wanted to end it all, there were funnel cakes.

Most riders skipped all the vendors and went straight into the huge greenhouse, knowing it would be empty of seedlings in July. The cathedral-like roof overhead created a large space filled with an intricate series of rafters and irrigation pipes. The far wall hosted several huge fans, four-foot tall each, reversed to blow inward. Bodies sprawled atop row upon row of empty tables, hot and steaming in the germination area like brightly-adorned pod people from outer space. A dozen hoses worked overtime, watering prone bodies or being held over heads for a shower.

Aaron and Cheek headed into the greenhouse while I purchased a bandana for my smarting head. I was used to road grit, but not road grit and sweat. The axiom of 'when you stop sweating, you're dehydrated' doesn't apply to biking in the Mojave Desert because sweat evaporates before your senses recognize it was ever there. But here my brow was actually wet. Soon I sported a stylish cow-spotted bandana.

I found Cheek sprawled upon a table beside Team Road Booty, a host of pretty ladies in bright orange bikini tops with matching mini-skirts over their chamois. Cheek had rolled over on the table, arm propped up and head resting in his palm, 'reading the text' of a sweat-soaked Team Road Booty mini-skirt. A bestseller, indeed. With dreamy eyes and a sly grin he asked, "Can we stay here for the rest of the day?"

But Aaron's attention was directed elsewhere. He was scrutinizing a load of steaming pasta he had obtained from Pastafari. Beneath a thick layer of grilled zucchini and squash, noodles glistened with olive oil and finely chopped basil.

"This is, this is excellent," Aaron said, motioning with his fork. "I'd heard Pastafari was started by a professional rider lamenting a lack of healthy food on the road. He nailed it."

"That looks great," I agreed. "How much?"

"Twelve bucks for a bowl of pasta and an orange juice," he answered.

"Pretty steep," Cheek dismissed.

"Not for quality like this," Aaron said. "This pesto is made fresh from basil obtained from farms on the road, twice as flavorful as stuff languishing in a store display for a week. Same with the vegetables: all farm fresh, not sprayed down with waxes and preservatives, not grown abroad and shipped in. Except the cheese: check this out! Imported, aged Italian parmesan on top —as much as you want—grated right from the wheel. None of that powdered, additive-heavy crap in a can."

"Mmph," Cheek replied, watching Team Road Booty walk away. "I heard they're going to a nearby town that opened up some hot tubs to riders. I can think of worse things than hot-tubbing with *her*."

"We're only halfway done," I pointed out. "We've had a few delays and are running kinda late. It's already two o'clock."

"You're such a party pooper," Cheek grunted.

Aaron set aside his empty bowl and laid back with a slight groan. With a chuckle he commented, "Brian used to be the life of the party."

"Yeah, but now I'm married," I joked.

"How you doin', Aaron?" Cheek asked.

"Ask me again after I resurrect," he replied. Flopping an arm over his head, he added, "*If* I resurrect."

Aaron did resurrect, as did Cheek. I did not share

the adverse effects of the heat with them, but certainly empathized. Compared to a June back home, this felt like early morning. But I kept my mouth shut—a real rarity, to be sure. I was proud of the boys and how they were handling it. Aaron, in particular, hadn't felt anything warmer than 65° for over ten months. Yet he voiced not a word of complaint. If the weather had been too cold for me—say, anything under 85°—there would have been no end to my whining. Nor did Cheek complain, though his behavior was decidedly less noble than Aaron's.

Everything changed in the next town. Things weren't going particularly easily on that first day, but they were about to get much, much more trying.

In Griswold, Cheek unleashed.

CHAPTER FIVE

Enter Cyclone

Griswold felt like the beginning of the end. At halfway through the first of seven days, this did not bode well.

Yet Griswold began well enough, cruising comfortably through several blocks of quiet neighborhood streets under venerable oaks. American flags fluttered over nearly every porch. With an estimated 120 armed forces veterans living therein— over 15% of the population—Griswold was a truly patriotic community. Inherently grateful as we three were at this, our more immediate gratitude was directed to the giggling boys in ball caps hosing down passing riders. Houses faded into small businesses and a main street formed. Riders loitered, crowds thickened, and defensive moves demanded focus. Slowing down in town was trickier than on the roadside because there was no clear shoulder for you to scamper onto before being nipped on the rear tire.

We stopped before a rather telling vacant lot. The neighboring building provided shade across only half the ground, a line of demarcation well noted by heat-beat riders. One half was a bright, blazing square void of life in the otherwise packed downtown, while the dark half was a seething mass of ruined riders squirming to escape the relentless heat. Complete with moans and sighs, the scene nicely illustrated Dante's *Inferno.*

"The heat's getting really bad," Aaron commented unnecessarily. He checked his iPhone and reported, "94 degrees and 80% humidity."

"That's not bad," I said mechanically, before I could stop myself. Two scathing looks rebuked me.

"But we've been going since 6:30," I offered as apology. "It's now four o'clock. That's a lot of cumulative heat."

"This is the next to last town, right?" Cheek said. "I'm getting a drink. We're *all* getting a drink."

"This isn't the next to last town," Aaron said.

"This is what you *do* at RAGBRAI," Cheek continued. "You drink. Check out all those bars on Main Street."

"I need a break, too," Aaron said nervously, "but it's not the penultimate town. It's getting late. I'm not sure we should take too long a stop."

Both men looked to me as arbiter, but I threw up my hands and joked, "I'm only here for the chicks."

"The bar then!" Cheek exclaimed triumphantly.

Aaron shot me a mildly perturbed look. I shrugged an apology.

Grudgingly we followed Cheek as he pushed his way through the crowds to a glass-fronted bar. The exterior of the structure conformed to the brick and glass facade of small towns everywhere. But for the faded Bud Light poster, it could have passed for a barber shop or five and dime. The sounds emanating from inside, however, made the establishment's purpose all too clear. Inside was pandemonium.

"I don't, I don't think this is a good idea!" Aaron shouted into my ear. "I'm too tired, it's too hot, and we've got too far to go!"

I could barely hear him above the noise. The place was a madhouse of bodies reeling from too much heat or too much drink. Probably both. Cheek's dark, handsome eyes flashed with excitement as he gazed around the overcrowded bar, to a back room like a can of sardines, and finally out the door to the patio from whence blared a live band. Aaron shouted at Cheek a couple of times, but it fell on deaf ears.

The sailor was in port.

Cheek leapt into the crowd and disappeared, setting off much as he did when returning to the ride. Aaron and I communicated by pantomiming a drink and pointing to the bar, behind which sat a refrigerator loaded with chilled Gatorade. Aaron slipped his way up to the bar to procure the elixir of life, then turned to see the sailor with his own recipe. There stood Cheek holding a frozen margarita in each hand, cheeks all puffed up and red with excitement, eyebrows raised so high they touched his hairline. I had never before seen a man so happy.

What can you do? We sat beneath the stuffed bison head with a Day-Glo green bra hanging over a horn. I was tempted to steal the garment to adorn my bike.

"Thanks, guys," Cheek screamed. "I needed a drink or three."

"Sure," Aaron mumbled, though it was lost to the oppressive music. Once Cheek had made the decision for us, however, Aaron seemed relieved to be taking a long rest.

"Oh," Cheek said, "You know how I said I trained on a stationary bike?"

"Lots of miles," I quoted. "On the hard setting."

"Yeah... not so much."

Before our very eyes Cheek downed both margaritas with sloppy, neck-pumping gulps, one after the other.

"You destroyed those margaritas," Aaron commented. "Most impressive."

Cheek's eyes flashed and he said to me, "*Proeliator modus.*"

Before we knew it, he was gone for more. Aaron appeared concerned. Our eyes met, and I finally had to ask the questions I'd been burning to all day.

"Who the Hell *is* this guy?" I shouted. "He's like a big, fuzzy dog. He wanders around aimlessly then suddenly focuses, like 'squirrel!' Except in his case it's 'muffin!' And, like a dog, whenever he finds a spot that's cooler he just stops and naps. Doesn't matter where it is, public, private, whatever!"

Aaron laughed and said, "True, but don't tell him that. He won't take it the way you mean it. He won't think you're joking."

"I'm not sure I am," I muttered.

"What?" Aaron cried over the noise.

"How do you know him?" I said, quickly moving on. "What's he do in the Navy?"

Aaron pondered a moment, then said, "I don't really know. Been trying to get that out of him for years. I know him as well as anybody, but don't know that. He was best man at my wedding. He was the one who forgot to put gas in my Prius on the way to town. He stranded the entire bridal party on the highway."

My eyes widened. "That was *him*?"

"Those emergency road-side phones are expensive!" Aaron continued. "But he's Johnny-on-the-spot in his professional life. When we lived together—I rented a room in his house in Monterrey when I first arrived in town—his attire was always neatly pressed and crisp, his demeanor sharp. He is superbly efficient and precise. Trust me, you've never seen someone so smart, except maybe Dad."

I sipped my Gatorade in wonder.

Aaron mused, only half-joking. "He might be a spook."

"A what?"

"A spook," he repeated. His voice was getting hoarse trying to communicate over the thundering music and drunken revelry. "A spy. I don't, I don't know for sure, but he's supremely secretive about what he does. Both Mom and Dad were in the military—Mom was even a Navy brat—and neither of them have ever seen someone as smoothly evasive as Cheek."

Cheek looked even less like James Bond than he did Maverick from *Top Gun*!

"All I know," Aaron continued, "is that when he's on leave, he shuts his brain off. So we indulge him."

But Cheek's indulging was just getting started.

After downing his two margaritas in record time, Cheek wandered drunkenly across the street to the general store and bought a jar of pickles. He stumbled back out into the heat to snarf down the whole thing. He fished around the brine with his dirty fingers until he gobbled every last pickle. I doubt he had time to even breathe during the operation. Then he threw his head back and glugged all that remained. Pickle juice poured down his unshaven cheeks. He wiped his whiskers with fingerless gloves. *'LOVE'* and *'HATE'*, stitched on the knuckles, stained sickly green.

A gross jersey sopping wet with sweat, dribbles of frozen margarita and now—worst of all—odiferous pickle juice. Hours more riding in the blazing hot sun of July. I couldn't imagine anything more awful. This was a failure of imagination. Cheek staggered back into the store and bought a liter of milk. Down the hatch, splashing more down the front of his jersey.

Two young men from Team Bike-sexuals happened by. One noted Cheek's Navy spandex and pointed to the Van Gogh pattern on his jersey. *The Starry Night* pattern, in an effort to stretch across Cheek's large belly, had swelled the stars into meteors that burst in a flurry of particles and mist.

"Ooh, look!" the man said flirtatiously to his companion. "A sailor and a late night explosion."

The joke fell flat when his partner observed Cheek's blank expression: fully margarita'd, pickled, and milked. He looked like a zombie that broke into someone's home and was killed by throwing everything in the kitchen at it. They hurriedly departed.

We needed to sober Cheek up for the remaining miles, of which there were many. Grudgingly we stalled another half an hour. Insisting on keeping Cheek on his feet, we toured a surprisingly interesting display of old combines, tractors, and antique farm tools. While Aaron and I browsed—lovers of history of all sorts—we eventually realized Cheek had disappeared. Frantically we searched, scanning crowds that were drinking, laughing, and napping.

After ten minutes we discovered Cheek had blundered into a museum of antique cars. He had claimed ownership of a display of an old-fashioned drive-in theatre. An antique Studebaker sat beside a pole offering a ruddy metal speaker designed to hook onto the car. Perched on the driver-side window was a wire tray featuring a faux cheeseburger, bottle of ketchup, and A&W root beer mug. Inside, on the leather bench seat lie Cheek, curled up and snoring.

After a few gentle touches, then a few not-so-gentle shoves, we roused the beast. Cheek rose up, eyes darting to take in the scene—probably wondering how he got there—even as he boldly exclaimed, "I'm ready for action!"

Happy to finally get a move on, we ushered Cheek to his bike and set off. We turned off Main Street, eager to leave the crowds and hit open road. We traversed a few blocks down a beautiful oak-lined residential street when suddenly Cheek's drive train malfunctioned. He fumbled a bit with his pedals to compensate. Not satisfied with the results, he kicked down. Hard.

SNAP!

Cheek's bike wavered like a boxer who'd just taken a knock-out blow, then staggered towards the curb. Cheek leapt off just as the broken bike tumbled to the ground.

"What the Hell was that?" I asked.

"Gearing's shot!" Cheek called back from the grass. He didn't seem upset, but rather excited at a moment of action.

Aaron groaned and lamented, "Would have been nice if that happened *before* our break."

Yet by blind, dumb luck Griswold's mechanical tent was not back on Main Street, but a mere 100 yards in front of us!

"Gearing's shot," repeated the bike mechanic moments later. "I'll need some time to replace it. I don't have one here, but can send someone for it. It'll take an hour just to get here."

"OK," Cheek said cheerily. He then laid down right there on the grass by the road and fell asleep.

"So much for going on ahead," I said to Aaron.

"Let's hope they don't close the roads on us," he replied, eyes lingering on his watch. He did not appear particularly amused.

So we waited. Cheek began snoring, and threw his arm over the curb so that it stuck out into the street. We moved it safely onto the grass a couple of times, but he kept throwing it back out. Finally we gave up, instead setting my glowing green bike in front of him as warning to passing bikes and cars. An *hour and a half* later, Cheek's bicycle was ready to be ridden again. We kicked him awake.

"Mmph," Cheek said. "Oh, you know how I said I took my bike to the shop while I trained on a stationary bike?"

We both waited.

"Yeah... not so much. Never even looked at it. Boxed it myself the mornin' I left."

I stared at him, aghast. "So the missing brake...?"

"Probably in my shed, home to spiders and such."

Hoping to catch up on time, we pushed through the next town. Lewis, population 438, boasted the world's largest bike. In honor of RAGBRAI, local Duane Weirich had welded together pipes and scrap metal to create a machine 15 feet high and 32 feet long. *'It's ridable!'* a sign boasted. How they could prove that was open to conjecture. Paul Bunyan, after all, was 500 miles north, near Fargo.

We grew very nervous about time, knowing the Iowa State Troopers stopped halting auto traffic at 6PM—which was *now*. Navigating highway traffic with a drunken Cheek did not sound fun. Alas, before we even risked that, Cheek prompted *yet another* delay. A large animal farm along the last highway offered a

200-foot water slide. Cheek simply had to do it. Unfortunately for Aaron, I did, too.

"We're already too late," Aaron warned when we pulled into the muddy yard at the roadside.

But Cheek just scoffed, asking, "How can you not do this?"

Aaron sniffed the air and his nose contracted in regret. Answer enough. He looked to me for support.

"Sorry, Aaron," I said regretfully. "But I gotta go with Cheek on this one. Late or not, a two hundred foot water slide is too much awesomeness to pass up."

I felt bad for Aaron, particularly because I understood his concern. I lived it. I was pathologically punctual for everything. Early, even. But this was an exhilarating 'screw it' moment. I usually lived for such moments, but had learned to squelch them by adventuring in the wastes of Nevada. Out there, people literally died from such foolhardiness. But not here. What could go wrong?

"We have, we have ten more miles to go!" Aaron gently insisted. "I can't get Dad on the phone. He probably thinks we've gotten lost. And we will be, too, because we don't know where he set up camp. We really don't have time for this."

But Cheek had already dropped his bike and was marching up the sloppy, grassy slope to the top of the slide.

"I'll wait here," Aaron finally said, defeated.

I hurried after Cheek, feeling like a gleefully naughty kid.

The farmer had created the huge slide by digging

a trench down a long, wandering slope between stables and barns. Sheets of plastic had been laid down and an irrigation pump loosed a torrent of water down it. At the top, beside a huge barn with aluminum siding radiating heat like the sun, we removed our helmets, shoes, and socks. Having forgotten to hand my money clip to Aaron, I instead placed it in Cheek's CamelBak. But, like all things Cheek, no simple task was easy as it should have been.

"I think this is more holes than bag," I grumbled, desperately seeking a pocket or corner not bereft of stitching.

"Fifteen years old," Cheek grunted, laboring with an unruly, sweat-soaked sock.

Inflated inner tubes lay in a pile near the irrigation pump. We chose our vehicles and threw ourselves into the chute. We zoomed downward. The world spun crazily, offering only glimpses of barns, cows, a silo, and miscellaneous farming equipment of dubious purpose. While slippery smooth, the trench was far from graded. Undulations shot us into the air, flying for heart-stopping moments with a surge of water, only to come splashing messily down.

At the bottom I slammed into a cluster of middle-aged ladies. They scattered like bowling pins. The cascade poured over us and built up a fair pond before seeping into the surrounding mud. We flopped about trying to disentangle ourselves, squealing joyfully as would any other pigs in the mud.

It was an immensely refreshing ride, but time was ticking. Forcing dry socks onto wet feet added to the delay. By the time I finished, I realized I was alone. Cheek's socks lay abandoned on the ground beside me. His helmet and shoes were gone and, more importantly, so was his CamelBak—with my all my money! I sloshed hurriedly back to the bikes, but Cheek was gone.

Aaron had been waiting impatiently by the bikes while we played on the water slide. He was still there, looking more frustrated than even when his bike broke down at the starting line.

"Where'd Cheek go?" I demanded.

"I don't know," Aaron answered. "I asked him how it was, but when I turned my back he vanished."

We glanced up and down the hills, but of Cheek there was no sign.

"How well do you know this guy?" I asked with a huff. "He's got all my money, my driver's license, and credit cards. Three hundred and fifty bucks buys a lot of pork chops, man!"

"It'll turn up," Aaron said helpfully.

But I was in no mood to forgive the ever-vexing addition to the Tire Dips. My complaints came hot and steady. "Yeah, it'll turn up on the roadside somewhere. I'm sure it'll fall out of one of the dozen holes in his crappy backpack. We'll never find it in all these weeds and ditches. After all his pressure to conform to his ideas of RAGBRAI, stalling like crazy and bullying us to do what he wanted, he ditches us. That's one helluva friend you got, Aaron."

Aaron was unperturbed by my outburst. He no

longer seemed perturbed at our incredible tardiness, either. In fact, he started laughing!

"At least, at least he didn't lose the rings on your wedding day!"

"You've got to be kidding."

"No, really. He was my best man, and I specifically told him 'don't ever let go of these'. They were custom made to Isabel's specifications. If you knew Isabel, you'd understand how exacting that process can be. But Cheek left them in the room and the stewardess took them."

"Unbelievable," I groaned.

"There were more than a few hours of panic, police, and more panic. Even made it in the police blotter. But he recovered them," Aaron continued. "Cheek's very resourceful. He gets things done."

I was dubious, but dropped it. I quickly apologized for my outburst.

"I'm sorry," I said. "I'm just used to being a loner. Guess I'm having trouble adapting."

"Cheek takes some getting used to," Aaron agreed, chuckling. "But really, I'm sorry about all this."

Onward we went. After all, we still had ten miles to go and it was 6:20PM. An hour later Aaron and I pedaled tiredly into the final town of Atlantic. The sun was slipping below the western hills and the cicadas sang merriment at approaching night. Their synchronized call resounded all around us, drowning out even the sounds of distant RAGBRAI revelry. Atlantic was a modestly large and prosperous town, host to a Coca Cola bottling plant. This made it a joy to wander, for each brick abode nestled snugly among fully established foliage was distinctly unique, distinctly beautiful. But we weren't in the mood for any of it. We just wanted to find Doc's camp, and the thick trees and growing shadows made it difficult. Numerous darkening signs directed riders to many locations, but none were for us. We passed the tent cities and just kept going mile after extra mile. Finally we stopped.

"Try the cell again?" I asked.

"No reception," Aaron said. "Though I just remembered Dad mentioning he'd made arrangements with the local medical community to park in one of their lots. Maybe we can find a medical center or something."

We asked some locals for directions to such, and were directed up the steepest, longest hill of the entire day. It easily added three hundred vertical feet to our day's already high tally. Atop the promontory spread a campus of one-level buildings surrounded by lush lawns and leafy trees. Alone in the parking lot was Doc's RV. The man himself spied us immediately and waved us over.

"You made it!" Doc greeted jovially. "I was starting to get a little worried."

"A few mechanical issues," Aaron said, plopping down into a chair.

"And a few Cheek issues," I added. "Any sign of him?"

"He's in the shower," Doc said. "Arrived about ten minutes ago."

"See?" Aaron mused, eyes closed in luxuriant rest. "I told you he's very resourceful."

"He better 'resource up' my money," I grumbled. Spying his broken CamelBak on the ground, I poked through it until I found my money clip. It was unscathed.

Thirteen-plus hours on the open road in the über-heat took its toll on all of us. Even when we had stopped for a rest in the shade, we couldn't help dwelling on the hours of riding ahead of us. Now that the first long day was done, we thought only of *days* more of it. If things were gonna be like this the whole week, especially with all the 'mechanicals', as Doc labeled them, I seriously wondered if we would make it.

We were happy for the quiet setting Doc had procured for our camp. From our vantage on the hilltop, the sunset was most inspiring. The rolling hills of happy green spreading to the horizon took their time darkening. A slight breeze eased the effects of the humidity, but still promised a hot, muggy night. While Aaron took his turn in the RV's shower, I set up my tent, shrugging off jokes about being a glutton for punishment.

"Enjoy the hot night while you can," Doc said. "Tomorrow we're assigned a spot in a crowded asphalt lot. I doubt you'll want to tent on that. You'll be forced to endure air conditioning."

Once cleaned up, we dined on a large salad. After a day of vendor food, its healthiness was most refreshing.

"Atlantic boasts some pretty wonderful pies," Doc said, munching on veggies. "I read that Chef Charlene Johnson's Sour Cream Raisin and Chocolate Peanut Butter Explosion pies have both won national honors. Did you guys have any pie today?"

Aaron had two slices of pie. Cheek had three. Nobody waited for me to say "none", assuming I was a health nut. They had yet to see me encounter pork. Doc asked in fatherly fashion, "Learn anything today?"

"Yes," Aaron said, pulling the leg of his shorts up to reveal half a thigh blazing red. "One layer of sunblock isn't enough."

To further demonstrate, he pulled up his shirt to reveal a funky red V down his chest.

"And don't unzip your jersey," he added. "Portland's had a particularly wet year, and I haven't seen the sun in ages. I feel good, though."

"I learned I probably overtrained—," I began, but was interrupted.

"You think?" Aaron teased.

"... but that's a good thing. No surprises for me. Then again, I discovered that painting my bike was a stroke of genius."

"You told the bike guy it was a moment of weakness," Cheek challenged.

"I'm no stranger to living in self-delusion," I admitted. "Vegas was founded on it. But today I literally heard at least seventy-five people comment on the bike. I never dreamed it would bring out a smile on so many faces. In Vegas it only brought sniffs of disdain."

"I heard at least a dozen comments as well," Aaron added. "You were the delight of children everywhere."

"My main aim in life," I snorted. Aaron knew I was too uptight to like kids.

"How about you, Cheek?" Doc asked.

But Cheek was gone. He had slipped away under cover of distraction. We spied him around the corner of the RV, secretly rubbing every inch of his body with some sort of horse liniment.

I awoke at 5AM, the birds my alarm. They chirped and fluttered noisily, excited at the imminent arrival of the sun. They'd have to wait a while, though. A thick mist spread across the land, tumbling roughly through the hills but smoothly mixing with the horizon. The wavy orb of day was veiled heavily by the mist's cherry glow. The crowns of hills rising above the fitful blanket were neat with rows of corn damp with dew. Tassels caught the red in their coarse, pale flowers, creating the illusion of orderly columns of flames laying siege to the town. When the breeze fluttered, fiery soldiers marched. Maybe that explained why the mist was so hot.

This was my idea of camping—waking in a medical center parking lot notwithstanding—waking for peaceful dawn, not for hectic morning habits. Most RAGBRAI participants camped en masse. Teams were assigned dense sites in school yards, football fields, city parks, or really any large area of grass. Walking amongst a camp of several thousand hung-over, body-aching, or belly-aching folks was certainly not communing with nature. Individual riders tended to fare better, sometimes being assigned the front yards of locals who had signed up as hosts.

I was really hoping to make a connection with Aaron today. Day 1 had not provided such an opportunity. That ride had been full of newness for us both, not to mention several breakdowns to contend with. But 'mechanicals' were to be expected.

Cheek suddenly kicked open the door of the RV. He filled his robust chest with a mighty intake of breath, then released it with a long, leisurely sigh—and stuffed a cookie in his mouth. Cheek most definitely was *not* to be expected in any way, shape, or form.

The fog rose, abandoning the valleys to smother hilltops in drab white blah. The tips of taller silos poked the cloud. Into such somber beauty we set off, leaving Atlantic and using a country highway to chase the hidden sun. Around us flowed rows of rich green corn and soybean, mingling with surprisingly large fields of wildflowers, their nickel-sized heads navy blue. Together the plants wove a quilt of colors that undulated away to the wall of hot mist at every horizon.

A soft morning promised a good day for contemplation, of conversation, a good heart-to-heart with an old friend. The promise was never fulfilled. Indeed, the day ended in nothing short of disappointment.

Yet smiles were to be had at the very first farm.

Perched at the roadside was a table, atop it percolating free coffee, behind it bubbling three children. Three very young girls, to be precise, with their mother and grandparents. While riders winced at delightfully scalding coffee, the girls sang, "Sign the sign! Sign the sign!"

On a tripod was a large sign reading, '*Please sign your name and hometown—it will be a geography lesson for the kids. Thanks!*' To grant extra credit I signed my wife Aurelia's name and Romanian home of Bucharest.

Then came the hills.

Within moments Aaron, Cheek and I were divided. Cheek powered up the first hill and was lost to sight, no doubt feeling he had something to prove. Aaron said he needed to take his time. It was evident he hadn't yet recovered from the previous day's heat. His sunburns itched and radiated heat of their own. He was in for a hard day: forecast was greater heat than before, as well as higher and longer hills. At least Days 3 and 4 promised relative flatness. But until then we'd have to wing it. Because of my over-training, it was actually harder for me to slow my pace when climbing hills, so I left him to his own devices. I understood his desire to not burden his friends, to face challenges alone. We agreed to meet in the first town and try from there.

Traveling alone let me observe more things RAGBRAI. Excellent communication was what first struck me. Everyone worked together for maximum safety, such as yelling 'rumble!' when encountering the disastrous grooves. A vehicle approaching from the oncoming lane prompted the cry of 'car up!', which rippled down the line as each rider repeated it for those too far back to see. Similarly 'car back!' was for a vehicle passing from behind. Unrepeated were noises of individual intention, such as a courteous shout of 'slowing'—we had no brake lights—or 'rider off' when pulling onto a shoulder. Things got comical under fatigue, but so automatic was the need for communication we would yell about anything on the road, such as 'water bottle up' or 'squirrel up'.

I began to casually poll riders about what, in their opinion, was RAGBRAI's No. 1 feature. I expected a litany of 'the beer!' or 'the pies!' The overwhelming answer, however, was 'the people'.

"It's like a family with one mission—to get across the state," mused a lady in a faded Penn State T-shirt. "Iowa's not as easy as I'd thought it'd be!"

"The shared pain and struggle is part of it," her husband chimed in. "That's what unites the RAGBRAI horde from around the globe. If a committee of tourism professionals built an effortless, politically correct ride like a theme park, it wouldn't be even half as much fun."

"RAGBRAI mirrors the human condition," opined a portly, retired man. "Oh, how we love to grouse about the trouble we've pedaled ourselves into—preferably over a cold beer in the next overnight town."

The most succinct comment came from a couple on their fourth RAGBRAI: "We're getting accustomed to being amazed every year."

I couldn't shake the feeling that more people were on the road that second day, despite having acclimated to crowded riding by then. Perhaps the dearth of 'breakfast farms' was explanation. The first town was about fifteen miles from Atlantic, which meant a little over an hour ride. As I neared civilization, the riders thickened and bunched beyond accountability. Elk Horn and its sister city, Kimballton, were chaotic, sprawling affairs. Good thing, that sprawl, because otherwise the sheer humanity simply could not fit.

A 163-year-old Danish windmill in Elk Horn greeted riders to the sister cities. Why such a sibling pairing was necessary out there in the middle of corn fields was a mystery to me, but maintain individuality they wanted, so maintain individuality they did. But their shared celebration of Scandinavian ancestry was evident. Together, the sister villages boasted the largest rural Danish community outside of Denmark.

I took it all in via signs, which was all that was left to me above the sea of helmets and roaring, crashing waves of crowds—other than the sixty-foot windmill, of course. Navigating among the masses soon became rather trying, but I went with the flow. I had to!

'Velkommen!' read the first. Hi, Elk Horn.

'Danish Immigrant Museum - Free tours!' offered the next. I was a museum junkie, but the pulsing crowd pushed me right on by. Maybe next time.

'Abelskivers!' advertised many. Queries to my jostling fellows revealed abelskivers as tasty little Danish pancake-popover hybrids. Though curious,

long lines deterred sampling.

'Kimballton has MERMAIDS!'

I stopped dead in my tracks. The tide of bikers flooded around me with angry mutters, but I didn't care. Now *this* was a thing to fight for! Shaking a fist with mock defiance at the windmill, I cried, "Screw your abelskivers, Elk Horn. I want mermaids. I'm going to Kimballton!"

And there they were, under a canopy: three lovely teenage mermaids in a wading pool. Beautiful smiles. Long hair loose upon bare, tanned shoulders. Bikini tops, naval rings, and tail-encased legs. I suddenly felt ashamed to have posed with lowly catfish.

A thick crowd of equally intrigued riders—all male—milled around the pond, pushing and shoving to be next in line for a photo with the ichthyological beauties. They were cheerleaders from the local high school, of course, raising money for charity by selling photos. For extra money, they let you doff your shoes and sit in the water beside them. I couldn't get my money out—nor my shoes off—fast enough. Yes, I labored under some naughty-cheerleader meets girl-next-door thoughts. After gleefully hurling away my socks, I hopped impatiently on the soggy ground.

My turn came and I all but leapt over the two-foot rim of the pool and waded out to the mermaids. One perched her hot pink tail upon a large boulder, while another wriggled her sea-blue length upon a shelf.

"One fish, two fish, pink fish, blue fish!" I babbled eagerly, plunking myself down on the shelf. "What's your name, dear?"

"Taylor," she answered, giggling at my enthusiasm.

Getting my flirt on, I was about to put my arm around her for the photo, when suddenly self-awareness intruded. Taylor was probably only sixteen years old and I was, like, *waaaay* over double that. Such was the first moment I realized I wasn't twenty years old since... well, since I was twenty years old. I was being the creepy old guy. I didn't want to be the creepy old guy. My shoulders drooped, sad, defeated, just as the photographer cried, "Say cheese!" The photo caught me slumped in disappointment, grinning, but weakly.

Perhaps even more readily apparent than my being old was that I'd never find Aaron in this mess of people. I decided to get breakfast for myself and hoped to meet him—or Cheek, I guess—in a less chaotic future town. I moved through the crowds, waiting to see what would catch my fancy.

Countless dogs ran through the streets of the Danish villages, nipping at heels as if people were cars. None appeared strays, but rather family dogs let loose for the action. I smiled in recollection of the previous day, when a huge, shaggy farm dog raced all over his huge front yard hill, running from biker to biker to biker, excited beyond imagining at all these new friends. Oh boy oh boy, look at *this* new friend. Oh, and *this* one! No doubt that night he slept twenty hours straight.

Regarding breakfast, I found myself swayed by the lungs of another teenage girl. Assigned to hawk the wares of a typical breakfast tent, she did so with gusto. Most impressive to me, however, was her wholesome approach. It obviously never even occurred to her to disparage the competition. The others weren't selling crap, but rather, "Ours is simply the BEST!" I was not alone in admiration for her honest, wholesome enthusiasm. A man in front of me whipped out a video camera and began interviewing her on the spot.

"Where you from?" he asked the vivacious, attractive lass of perhaps fifteen or sixteen. A bright red ball cap struggled to contain bushy brown hair. Her answer rang with even more pride and devotion than cheerleading scrambled eggs.

"I'm from ANKENY!" she blurted. "This isn't ANKENY. ANKENY'S by Des Moines. ANKENY didn't get to host RAGBRAI this year, but I'm cheering for next year. So come back next year, 'cus ANKENY's great!"

Perhaps not surprisingly, the breakfast was delicious. Even Aaron would agree that the tastiest ingredient is always love.

But the waves of riders kept coming, faster and more violently. It was time to depart, lest I be swamped. The 'cooling' mist had burned off. I used the word 'cooling' most carefully, for everybody else complained it was like a steam room. The dog days howled their preeminence. Needing water to make it to the next town, I stopped at the nearest such vendor. There I was struck by a most adorable moment.

A little girl, perhaps five or six, was selling bottles of water. A gentle, bookish man with greying hair ordered one. Small arms plunged shoulder-deep into a bucket of icy water to fish out a bottle. She held out the dripping item with both hands, when the man asked her, with a wry smile, "Has this water been obtained using the reverse-osmosis method?"

She paused, mouth hung open to reveal huge front teeth. Her face frowned in utter confusion, round cheeks turning bright red. "Huh?" she asked, bewildered, adorable.

I ached for a camera to capture that look, perfectly showcasing a child's lack of any sort of containment. I see it still crisply in my mind, but wish fervently to share it. If *that* wasn't a RAGBRAI moment, I couldn't imagine what was.

CHAPTER SIX

The Mystery of Templeton

RAGBRAI is an opportunity to expand one's horizons. An odd statement, considering it crosses what most Americans derisively call a 'boring' state. Foolish strangers, with all that pie—or beer—how can any lesson be boring?

Crossing Iowa by bike showcased a living history lesson of the American dream. The ideal that anyone can come to America and, with hard work, improve their life resonated in every community. The names of the towns hinted at this, such as Elk Horn or poor, flooded Hamburg. These were places where immigrants chased and cherished the American dream, even as they paid respect to their ancestry. Elk Horn's huge Dutch windmill was a brilliant example, but paled in comparison to the next town's pride: a 300-year-old German hausbarn brought over from the mother country.

Manning got their collective hands on the hausbarn in 1991. Apparently the Germans of the Schleswig-Holstein region felt a career of 331 years was not enough for the combination house and barn, for they refused to let it retire. Instead it was dismantled and sent to Iowa. Professional thatchers came with it, volunteering to rebuild the mighty roof in the traditional manner, bringing with them reeds grown near the Baltic Sea. Only Germans could engineer dried sticks into a roof ready to withstand Iowa winters for seventy-five years. But they knew exactly what was necessary, for the settlers of Manning had all come from Schleswig-Holstein and found it reassuringly similar to their north German home.

Such was the mutual pride of both parties that the Iowa groundbreaking ceremony was attended by none other than Her Highness Princess Elisabeth. Elisabeth, as we all know, is princess consort to the head of the Ducal House of Schleswig-Holstein-Sonderburg-Glücksburg, Christoph, Prince of Schleswig-Holstein. Duh.

I was impressed enough by the tour to support their efforts with an overpriced postcard, which I sent to Aurelia. At the hausbarn I also enjoyed a rare, calm moment watching an old man sitting on a bench, quietly regarding the blooming flowers. I couldn't remember the last time I had done such a thing, and felt a bit humbled by it. A beautiful moment, just for him—and, subsequently, for me.

Alas, it was the only moment of tranquility in that

boomtown-for-a-day. For there I discovered the extra day riders numbered over *5,000*. Manning's population of 1,500 was crushed by *ten times* as many people rushing through, and that still didn't even count the extra support staff, family, and friends for all of them. Extra day riders were not uncommon, but this volume was unprecedented.

So why *were* there so very, very many extra riders for the day? Because Des Moines, the capital was nearby? Couldn't be. To sample the homemade bratwurst and German potato salad? Not so much. For the full experience of beer-sauerkraut-fudge cupcakes? Most definitely not. No, I just couldn't figure out the reason for all the riders.

Manning wanted to be a town to remember. Months of planning had been devoted to creating RAGBRAI-centric attractions, such as the corn maze. The local Muhlbauer family, with help from LeRoy and Freda Dammann, had plotted the design with GPS, double-planted corn rows just fifteen inches apart, mowed paths clear, and finished the details with bean hooks and corn knives. The result of all this labor was the RAGBRAI XXXIX logo framed by a map of Iowa, filling up three acres of corn. At noon they took an aerial photo of thousands of riders filling the rows— more numerous than the corn itself, it seemed. Noteworthy as all that may have been, it was not nearly as impressive as the crowds.

Finding Aaron was out of the question. Finding breakfast was, too. Vendor lines were absurdly long, snaking all the way out of downtown. Everything from pancakes to pies required at least a forty-minute wait. More, if it looked particularly good, such as the bacon burrito line. There, impatient, hungry riders had already waited half an hour and were barely halfway through. It was enough to make me cry. Looked like the vendors wanted to cry, too, but they were too busy.

As soon as I spied a line only twenty riders deep, I jumped on. I didn't care what was offered, I just wanted to get something, anything, and get away from the mob. Even a beer-sauerkraut-fudge cupcake was welcome. Amidst the shifting, impatient mass of bodies, I began to feel claustrophobic. The radio blared warning:

"Sweltering humidity throughout this period will produce heat index readings from 110 to 115 degrees across much of the area each afternoon and evening. Warning: several days of dangerously high heat and humidity with little relief at night can cause significant physical stress and create conditions favorable for heat related problems. Stay indoors with air conditioning."

But I wasn't in air conditioning. I was stagnating in line for I didn't know what. My foolishness was soon proven complete: the line wasn't for food at all, but temporary tattoos.

So I got corny, if you pardon the pun, and chose an Iowa tattoo for my calf. As a rule I avoid bringing attention to my chicken legs, but was no doubt inspired by all the riders who wrote 'virgin' on their calves to show their excitement at joining RAGBRAI. I asked the vendor if my leg hair would get in the way, but his answer was merely a verbal "zzzz!", even as he rubbed an electric razor down my leg. A warning would have been nice.

All around me people grumbled, albeit good-naturedly, about how hot and muggy it was. I shrugged at that. Once free of the line, to me the air felt clammy and almost cool. Heat index of 110? That was *literally* my patio at 7AM every morning four months a year. But the smothering crowds concerned me greatly. How much extra, unrecorded heat was created by the dense crowds? Even if it was all mental, it was starting to freak me out.

I hated crowds, and this was the mother of all of 'em. The biggest crowd I'd ever seen was New Year's Eve on the Las Vegas Strip, where 320,000 revelers—that's visitors, *not* including any of the two million locals—flocked to the street. But that was spread out over dozens of casinos, each with enough rooms to hold three times the entire population of Manning. No, this was different. This was bursting at the seams in an unsightly way, like Big Elvis in only size 54 sequined pants. I had to get the Hell out of there. So out I got: hot, hungry, and tattooed. Not the way I liked to be, even if that's how I liked women.

Outside of town, I excitedly stopped at the Pastafari vendor. Finally, no lines! But there was a reason for that. For some ungodly reason they had set up their tent a mere hundred feet from a huge, industrial-sized pig barn. The smell was atrocious. Even the vendors themselves plugged their noses as they chopped squash. Stomachs roiling from distaste trumped grumblings from hunger, and not for just me: they'd hardly sold anything all morning. But salvation came soon, in the form of Mr. Pork Chop.

Halfway down the next hill was an old school bus. Entirely filling a gravel driveway, the pink vehicle—complete with pig ears and painted curly tail—nosed right up to the old farm house. It was easily spotted from half a mile away. Plumes of rapturous smoke billowing to the sky advertised heaven from even further afield. Yet this was earthly divinity, wrought by hard-working men sweating over massive, custom-made grills. The church of pork had a full and enthusiastic congregation.

Apron-clad men labored to flip racks of chops for even heating, to pour a smoke-enhancing elixir over the flames, or ready coals for yet another grill. Each grate roasted no less than a dozen dozen Iowa chops, each of the 144 treasures nearing an inch and a half thick, licked by flames and caressed by delicious smoke. It was truly an awe-inspiring sight. Overcome with joy, I hugged the bus.

"I did the same thing," the rider in front of me said when I danced into line.

"POOOORRRKK CHAAAAHHHHPPP!" came the cry of a passing rider.

That sounded familiar. Suddenly I recalled the bizarre wail I heard yesterday with Cheek. The ululating cry rose in volume and timbre until nearly ear-splitting... then slowly faded. But this was no Doppler effect. Dozens of others chimed in: riders riding, riders *waiting*. They sounded like a pack of wolves baying at the moon.

"What the Hell...?" I breathed.

"*That*, my friend," explained the rider before me, "Was the call of Mr. Pork Chop. His call was famous throughout all RAGBRAI-dom. He's retired now, but his spirit lives on."

"Extraordinary," I murmured. "I thought it was an ambulance."

"I wanted Pastafari today," the rider beside me commented, "but it's too early for pasta."

"Yet never too early for a pork chop," I agreed, only mildly distressed by how Cheekish that sounded.

"Thank you," said a passing man wearing a pink Mr. Pork Chop T-shirt.

"The owner," the rider said, nodding after the man. "The original Mr. Pork Chop's retired. That's his son."

"A good son," I complimented appreciatively. Though waiting in a long line *again*, my impatience lessened with every puff of wind that wafted the scent of roasting pork over me.

Finally a smoked, glistening pork chop of magnificent stature was handed to me, presented in a napkin. Nothing else was needed: no condiments, no salt and pepper, no knife and fork. It was a self-contained chop of perfection. I held it up to my nose to inhale the aroma, brought it to my lips to feel the heat upon them. Finally, savoring every millisecond of the process, I bared my teeth and sunk them in. The flesh was soft, juicy, delicious. Divinity on a bone.

Lost in the moment, I drifted away onto a hill,

into solitude. I wanted to be alone with that pork chop, so powerful were my emotions; the ecstasy of satisfying a hunger deep as my soul, the selfishness of wanting it all to myself. Aaron may be the foodie, but he'd be hard-pressed to beat one of these beauties.

Eventually I returned to earth. I was standing beside a sign that read *'one day old piglets'*. At my feet was a small enclosure of the little fellows. They were insanely cute. Sure, they'd grow up looking messy, but as babies they were bright pink and squirming and lively. Delighted adults waited to pet them, perhaps with less patience than even for lunch. Yet there I stood, munching on their brethren. I wasn't sure if I should feel guilty or not. Aurelia grew up eating her own pigs, and she didn't feel one whit of guilt. Grateful to resolve that moral dilemma, I munched on.

Nearby the trim owner dropped heavily onto a folding chair. He removed a white straw hat with a pig-pink band to wipe his forehead. I approached to compliment him.

"No postcards?" I asked.

"What?"

"Nothing. This is my first Mr. Pork Chop, and I must say it's fully deserving of its reputation."

"Thank you," he said earnestly. "Today's been a tough one already. I'm glad it's working out."

"Too hot?" I asked.

"It's always two hundred degrees over the grills," he pointed out. "No, we got a late start. Almost didn't get a location at all."

"I think Pastafari could learn something from

you," I offered.

The owner chuckled.

"I got a call from them late last night," the handsome man said. "They asked for help finding a new spot, since their old one cancelled at the last minute. Some church function, they said. We compete, but work together, you know? I like what they're bringing to RAGBRAI. They got their start as riders themselves, so they knew what was missing. Good for them. But I don't know how business savvy they are. The whole church function line was the farmer's way to ask for money. They wouldn't pay a dime, and look where they are today."

"You have to pay a lot for sites, then?" I asked, curious but not wanting to pry.

"Location is everything," he said. "We put a lot of thought into it. At the top of the hill everyone is exhausted and a pork chop sounds too heavy when you're panting. At the bottom everyone wants to use their momentum to get up the next hill, which trumps everything else. Halfway down the hill has its problems, too. People are just getting up momentum. But at least this way we weed out the non-serious pork eaters."

"Can't have those now," I said, tearing the last bite from the bone.

"But no, we usually don't pay a lot for our sites. We perform a service for the farmers by removing all their corn cobs."

"Corn cobs?"

He jerked a thumb over to the bus. Only then did

I truly see how customized their pink vehicle was. The majority of windows had not been boarded over simply to make it look pig-like, but rather to create a giant portable bin. Custom-built doors opened along the side to reveal heaps of corn cobs. Workers jabbed shovels inside and carted off full loads, which they dumped into the iron box grills.

"Free fuel," he explained. "On a good day we sell eight thousand chops: that'd be a lot of charcoal. Corn cobs give a nice smoky flavor, too. It's a win-win."

"POOOORRRKK CHAAAAHHHHPPP!" cried another rider.

"There goes my alarm," the owner said, rising slowly to his feet. "Break's over. Thanks for stopping. Enjoy your ride."

Back to work for me, too. Any hope of meeting up with Aaron was utterly gone. An afternoon lacking Cheek didn't bother me so much. Alone I rode.

The next town was Aaron's most anticipated, though I couldn't remember why. He had dreamed about visiting Templeton, which I thought a strange fascination for a man such as he. Scanning the vacant storefronts of the old main street with a frown, I was even more confused. The emptiness of the structures, some of old brick but most of modern siding, did not appear due to Sunday nor even RAGBRAI, but rather a fatal lack of revenue. The hot sun hammered the empty, extra-wide street, giving the lonely expanse a sense of desolation. Around the far corner a park filled with massive trees promised escape from the unresponsive, cemetery-like business district.

Riders flowed through the center of the wide street, but did not bring the aspect of life to this place. None slowed down, nor even looked around, but were intently focused on reaching the merciful shade of the distant park. I scanned their number for Aaron, but he could easily have been one of the thousands who'd beaten me to Templeton. I stopped in the sun beside a rusted 100-year-old car, parked incongruously before a plastic storefront. Beside it was a contemporaneous truck, upon the wooden flatbed of which were two barrels. I pondered whether or not they were clues to Templeton's secret. But many small Midwest towns offered such antiques.

The park enticed with shade and refreshments, but also crowds. To refresh myself there meant giving up on meeting Aaron. So I waited out in the open, hoping to spot or be spotted. I didn't mind waiting in the sun, since I was used to living under a broiler. Still, just because I was used to heatstroke didn't mean I invited it. After an hour it was time to move on. I may have missed his passing, but surely he would have seen the green machine glowing like plutonium. Disappointed, I moved onward.

Something made me not want to leave Templeton just yet, however. Perhaps it was the mystery. What about this place had made Aaron so excited? I wracked my brain for the memory, but it eluded me. The last mention of Templeton he made had been yesterday, in Griswold—at the little grocery store, of all places. He had squawked the words 'Templeton' and 'dusty', but beyond that I couldn't recall. I had been too horrified by Cheek's chugging of pickle juice and milk. A clue was offered on my way to the vendors, who had set up in the park. Upon the tall fences surrounding the adjacent baseball diamond were a series of metal placards.

'Many jugs ready for retail were stored in post holes at Templeton. Knowledgeable people could tell where liquor was hidden by observing the height of certain fence posts.'

Aha! Pieces of the puzzle were falling into place. The second sign confirmed it.

'Deputy United States Marshall Frank Thiede of Fort Dodge Saturday was ordered to destroy several hundred gallons of alcohol seized in recent raids by Federal investigators.'

That explained the old vehicles: they were 1920s-era. But why would Aaron be so interested in some small town's history, especially as it related to a neighboring town's current grocery store? Though happy to discover some new trivia, I was annoyed the full story still eluded me. I would simply have to learn about it later. Somewhat diffidently I wandered along the line of vendors. I spied something that seemed too down-home American to pass up: root beer floats. Wasn't ice cream always supposed to make one feel better? I usually leaned on rum, but a root beer float felt more appropriate.

They had quite an operation going. The rows of six-foot tables were an assembly line of old fashioned goodness. Burly men were in charge of scooping the rock-hard ice cream from the five-gallon tubs. On the next table the ladies poured in the frothy root beer. Finally, at the third table kids took money and gave out the necessaries, such as napkins, straws, and spoons.

But the real action unfolded behind the line of scrimmage. A long farm trough was filled with ice water and floating tubs of ice cream. A boy rushed back and forth along its length, reaching elbow-deep with latex-gloved hands to brush and prod clumping ice from the tubs. A little girl was supposed to be helping him, but she was too busy blowing up her glove into a balloon. A 15-year-old girl snapped at her, "Get to work! Go help at the front table!"

As soon as the overseer turned away, the little girl made a face at her back. Then, absently chomping on her tongue through the difficult process, she tied off her glove-balloon. Armed with this tool, she marched up to the front table to assist—not the people, but rather a box of plastic spoons. She pushed the inflated fingers into its contents, rattled the utensils around, and intoned, "A helping hand..."

She was entertaining herself quite well. And us. That is, until the 15-year-old saw her. Another squawk and the little girl was back to helping the boy in the trough, sighing heavily.

Just as I was about to leave Templeton entirely, Aaron spied me riding past. He flagged me down, shouting, "Hey, Big Green!"

I struggled to pull into a burgeoning crowd of exiting cyclists. The flow of bodies from the road was huge. Many streamed towards a small building of industrial design. At a second glance, however, I saw it was much larger than I had initially thought. Green aluminum roofing angled down over brown aluminum siding in various sections, some one story, others much higher. A wooden porch made a homey facade. I squinted over the milling crowd to the building's sign, but it was obscured.

"Hey, Aaron," I greeted. "What's that?"

"The distillery," he answered. "Templeton Rye. It's one of the best I've ever had. I just finished the tour."

"Ah!" I said, finally understanding. "*That's* what had you so hot and bothered about Templeton. Whiskey!"

"You don't remember me going nuts back in Griswold?" he asked.

"I remember Cheek going nuts back in Griswold," I deadpanned.

"That, too," Aaron agreed. "But while he was busy chugging pickle juice and milk, I saw in the little store five dusty bottles of Templeton Rye—five! It was more than I had ever seen in my life. There's a waiting list for it in Portland."

"You're kidding!" I exclaimed. "For whiskey made in Iowa? We're not exactly known for our whiskey prowess."

"Seriously," Aaron answered. "I asked the rep about it. He said they only use four distributors for the whole country: two in the Midwest, one in San Francisco and another in New York. Apparently the locals of Griswold didn't know they were sitting on gold. I wanted to buy all five bottles on the spot, but didn't have any way to carry them. Cheek's backpack is full of holes."

"Whiskey made in Iowa," I repeated, shaking my head in disbelief.

"It's seriously high quality stuff," Aaron explained. "They started in 2007 after extensive research. They were inspired by the early bootleg rye that was so famous—it was an open secret that Al Capone favored Templeton Rye during Prohibition. They got the original Kerkhoff family recipe that uses a mash of more than 90% rye. The rest is malted barley. Today's ryes only need 51% to be called rye, so that's a *huge* difference. I saw the 300 gallon copper still and a giant rack of aging barrels. There were about 150. I don't know why, but I find old wooden barrels to be beautiful."

"*That* I understand," I said. "They're usually filled with booze."

"I talked, I talked to a rep from the distillery," Aaron continued. "He said they allocated eighty bottles for free shots, but they ran out at 10:15 in the morning."

I shook my head in wonder.

"Anyway, if we get separated, don't wait. I may tour a winery that's a little out of the way."

"This really isn't fair," I commented, wistfully staring to the horizon. "Fine wines, fine scotch. How come Iowa is suddenly taking care of *your* interests? I'm still waiting to find a Cuban torcedor on some side street to roll me a fresh habano cigar."

Aaron and I did indeed get separated again. I had only spent about ten minutes with him all day. It was frustrating, but he was obviously having a grand ol' time without me. I had difficulty imagining how that was possible. Maybe my ex-wife had been on to something after all.

Eventually I passed a sign that said we had reached the highest point on the ride, at 1,491 feet elevation. *'All downhill from here!'* it read. That was a stretch, if well intentioned. But at least I no longer rode alone. In the tiny town of Dedham I had met up with a man from Quebec. His name was Adrien. After striking up a conversation at a fire hydrant turned water station, we decided to ride together awhile.

"You know what impresses me the most?" said the slender middle-aged man. Adrien's speech was a pleasant mix of fluent English with a light French accent. "Your policemen."

"Why's that?" I asked.

"I figured—as does most of the globe," he was quick to add, "that American policemen are all gun-blasting, profanity-spewing brutes."

"You watch too much TV," I lightly rebuked.

"Yes," Adrien agreed, smiling. "But look how helpful they are! I passed a railroad crossing earlier and saw them laying rugs over the tracks. How very courteous! I see them—not the local gendarmerie, but the intimidating looking ones with the bullet-proof vests—"

"Iowa state troopers," I supplied.

"Yes, them. I see them holding off traffic at all the intersections. The riders all thank them as they pass, though I don't think they hear. Their cars have doors open and radios playing loud rock music."

"Always AC/DC," I observed. "Or maybe Pat Benatar. It's the exact same music I listened to when I lived in Iowa as a kid. Kinda freaks me out, to be honest. I've heard more Styx in the last two days than I have in the last two decades."

As if on cue, we neared another intersection where two state troopers directed traffic. Sure enough, their idling squad car had doors open to blare *'Highway to Hell'* from AC/DC. I tried not to dwell on the appropriateness of the song. The troopers stood on the highway, chatting idly as they waved the horde of bikers around a corner.

"Ride between them!" someone shouted.

Suddenly a line of bikers broke from the pack and veered towards the authorities, intent on the three-foot gap between the men. Both troopers panicked and scampered out of the way. Once safely on the shoulder, they roared with laughter at their own behavior. The feint had been fun, but I doubted anybody'd have the guts to actually pull off a prank like that between troopers fully geared up with Kevlar and armed with Glock handguns!

In keeping with the musical era, we passed a rider hauling a full-sized speaker hooked to an iPhone blasting Journey's *'Open Arms'*. Inspired by the song, and perhaps his French background, my Quebecer companion exclaimed, "And RAGBRAI is so very romantic!"

I shook my head. "I may have been swept off my feet by Mr. Pork Chop, but that's something else entirely. Though it's true the mosquitos have been insistently amorous."

Adrien easily proved his point. He motioned to the very next rider, whose bike boasted a placard beneath the seat. "Look at that!"

The placard read *'I met my wife on RAGBRAI '96. Married 10 years, June 2007.'* Upon inquiry the proud husband flipped the placard over to reveal a wedding picture and portraits of a smiling boy and girl.

"If this is not a love story," Adrien said, "I don't know what is. RAGBRAI is full of superlatives, yes—biggest, longest, oldest—but it's the small, tender moments that matter. Like life, eh?"

He then pointed ahead of us, indicating two young ladies holding hands as they coasted down a long hill, obviously very much in love. We followed them into a drive-thru bike shower set up along the roadside by a particularly kind and industrious homeowner. The ladies slowed down so much in fear of striking the support poles that their bikes wiggled alarmingly. But they burst through the shower unharmed; relieved, refreshed, and laughing. Their glee was contagious.

Adrien and I parted in the town of Willey. This was a tiny town, population only 88. He was intent on romancing himself a 'world famous bologna on a stick', whereas I decided to remain celibate. I paused for a while at the particularly large and particularly lovely St. Mary's Catholic Church. The massive brick structure rose high on its own, but filling an entire hilltop made it doubly dominating. Rolling slopes behind were graced by a vineyard and several brick domiciles. A hundred yards away, past a surprisingly vast gravel parking lot, was a gargantuan beer tent. I chose to hover in front of the church and watch the nuns selling popsicles.

A tiny elderly nun in grey habit and white scapular smiled broadly as she handled transactions. Her wrinkled countenance shone healthy and bright with joy. She was having a grand time. In an amusing role reversal, her partner—a tall, very young nun— looked far more staid. She stood ramrod straight and fulfilled her duties with a quiet modesty that seemed most out of place in the celebratory atmosphere. Still, with each cherished frozen treat delivered she also gave a reserved smile. Amusingly, if the elder nun suspected the young sister was watching, she assumed the severe look that was the nightmare of schoolchildren everywhere. Both wore shiny new Birkenstocks.

I waited an hour at Willey, the penultimate town of the day's ride, but never caught sight of either Aaron or Cheek. Finally I had just gone on to the overnight town of Carroll. Because we had been assigned to the RV parking that night, finding Doc was easy. Numerous signs pointed the way to a school parking lot densely packed with RVs. As usual, Doc sat outside in the shade reading his Kindle.

"My, you're early," Doc commented, setting aside his reading. He wiped the sweat from his brow and regarded me a moment. Finally he quipped, "What, me sweat?"

"More like 'what, me shower?' I am in serious need of a carwash."

He smiled. "Have you seen anybody doing so?"

"Not yet," I said. "Though I understand it's quite common. It was hard to see anything through the crowds, though. Today was crazy!"

"An extra 5,000 day riders at least, so says the radio," Doc agreed. "That's a fifty percent increase."

"Proximity to Des Moines?"

"Proximity to a seven time Tour de France winner," Doc explained. "Paper said Lance Armstong's riding this leg."

Understanding blossomed. No wonder it had been so crazy today. My nemesis of Lance wanna-bes had been replaced with Lance wanna-sees!

That evening the four of us drove to downtown Carroll, touted by boastful signs as 'nouveau Las Vegas'. I threw up a little in my mouth.

"At a huge beer tent in Templeton firemen were hosing off hot dancers," I commented. "I sense that's more 'nouveau Las Vegas' than anything little Carroll has to offer. Just guessing."

Disdain for the moniker does not mean I wasn't impressed, however. The town appeared tremendously prosperous, with huge, gorgeous homes the envy of any of the nation's McMansion-dwellers. We were all astounded by their size and variety, but even more so by their numbers. We couldn't fathom how such a small town generated so much wealth. The downtown provided no answer to this mystery. It was not some hub of industry, but merely several sprawling blocks of mixed structures. It had a very open feel; an equal mix of green space, parking space, and office space.

Intent on Mexican food, we were delighted at the appearance of Rancho Grande with its delightful cantina-style patio dining. Alas, it was not to be. The line of hustling folks trying to get in was only surpassed by the jostling crowd of folks trying to pay, with only one lonely and utterly overwhelmed hostess between them. She nearly collapsed under the weight of it all. If cell phone towers were overloaded, the local restaurants stood no chance.

We eventually dined at a winery/restaurant combination offering a special buffet. Rather, they *had* offered a buffet. At merely 7PM they were closing their doors, food inventory exhausted. Desperate for non-vendor food, Doc managed to negotiate our entry, but under the strict understanding that we would only get one pass through the buffet. The host appeared dismayed at letting anyone see his work after being plundered by a hungry barbarian horde. He need not have worried, for his recipes were surprisingly industrious and most delicious. Aaron was impressed, which said much. Cheek somehow wrangled two extra plates of pasta before they shooed us away.

After dining quickly, we slowed down to enjoy some local wine. I knew next to nothing about wine, but it received a stamp of approval from the wine savvy Aaron and Doc. At one point, a sorry-looking rider came ambling up nervously. He nodded a sweaty, road-grimed forehead towards an uneaten plate of pasta in the center of the table.

"I hate to ask this," he said, wringing his hands in embarrassment, "but are you going to eat that? The owner let me in for free, saying I could eat whatever I found left. There's nothing."

Cheek slid the plate over with a smile. "I haven't touched it, sir. By all means."

The man gratefully accepted the plate, adding with a tired grin, "Even if you had, I wouldn't care at this point. I'm starving!"

"This is excellent wine," Doc remarked, bringing us back to the topic at hand.

"I did a quick tour of the winery," Aaron said. "Looked quite nice. I can't tell you how happy I am that Iowa is heading in the direction of the artisanal. It's like the 'new Iowa' that wasn't there when we were young. Suddenly Iowa is cool: microbreweries, wineries, artisanal foods. You know Dad, like La Quercia you introduced me to who makes traditional prosciutto. People in these small towns are really trying to do something innovative and new. I was looking forward to Templeton, but am happy to discover all kinds of little things around the state. In fact, there was even a local farmer giving out free bacon from a heritage breed of pig."

"Free bacon!" Cheek and I exclaimed simultaneously.

"What breed?" Doc asked.

"Does it matter?" Cheek interjected. "It's free bacon!"

"Berkshire," Aaron answered with a smile. "He wanted to stand apart, so imported English hogs. I was impressed. The distillery was impressive, too. The taste they gave us on the tour was astonishingly good. It was only half an ounce, but there's just something about scotch fresh from the barrel that bottles cannot capture. It was the best I've had since leaving Islay."

"I didn't know you went to Scottish distilleries," Cheek said, surprised.

"Yeah, he's done that, too," I remarked drily.

"I'll bet that set you back a lot," Cheek said.

"Not really," Aaron said. "This was when I was in college at Nottingham, so I was already close. It was before the whole tourism thing happened, so a lot of them didn't even have visitor's centers. I'd just walk up and knock on their doors. They'd take a break and show me around."

"That's amazing!"

"I rented a bike on the mainland at Oban," Aaron continued. "Then took a ferry to Islay. The next ferry back wasn't for a week, so I had lots of time. I rode all over and got into everything. Everybody knew each other, which meant they all knew me pretty fast. They even offered me rides in the back of their trucks. When you're twenty people are nicer to you than when you're forty. I got to know a lot of sheep rather intimately."

"Jeez," I commented. "That's straight out of *An American Werewolf in London*. At the opening the two guys were getting a ride in the back with the sheep...?"

"Hope you stayed off the moors at night," Cheek added with a grin.

Aaron laughed. "Yeah, yeah I forgot about that. It was just like that, too. Cloudy and cold, rolling hills and a bunch of sheep. Pubs go quiet when a stranger enters and everything. Actually, once I *did* get caught on the moors. The rain caught me and there was nothing but a sheep shelter. I squatted among the sheep for hours. I never told anybody that, scared I'd lose my cool factor."

"It doesn't hurt," Cheek said. "Just ask Brian."

After giving Cheek a sour look, I promised to Aaron, "Your coolness will be irrefutable when we make it to the Mississippi."

"As if you're an authority on the subject," Cheek grunted dismissively.

"We're having trouble getting the word out," I agreed gamely.

"Yet it's not for lack of trying," Cheek trumped.

Back at the RV we sat outside in the dark. The others enjoyed the nose of Templeton Rye while I puffed up pungent clouds of cigar smoke. This was wise on my part, for mosquitoes avoided me. The others were not so lucky. Nothing's worse than slapping sunburned flesh bitten by a mosquito. The sensory and physical overload of the day was behind us. We were tired, but not quite ready to retire. We had yet to process the day. Sounds of surrounding revelry rolled over us in occasional waves, like thunder from a distant storm, but the night was predominantly quiet.

The clink of ice in tumblers. Reflection, sharing. Humidity, bugs.

"Going up a long hill," Aaron offered softly, "a boy was blazing up past everyone. Someone managed to shout, over the puffing and blowing, 'how old are you?' The kid looked back and shouted with pride, 'I'm eight!' and kept on going. Groans of envy swept through the ranks."

"Day rider," we all called in unison.

"Did you see the bananacycle?" Cheek offered. "A couple made a huge banana frame around their tandem bike, easily ten feet long."

"I saw a pretty charming tandem today," I added. "There was dad and his little girl wearing a helmet with a huge butterfly glued to it. At the end of a long, hard day she was literally sleeping in the back, her little body slumped forward, head resting on hands resting on handlebars, while dad peddled on."

"If you're wondering why I arrived an hour later than the rest of you," Cheek suddenly piped up, "it's because I stopped at the rec center in the first town. They opened their pools and I swam there for over an hour. Only then did I realize I still had sixty more miles to go!"

Doc smiled into his rye, then changed the subject. "Tell me, Cheek, what do you do in the Navy?"

"Oh, different things depending on where I'm stationed," he answered distractedly. Joints cracked as he leaned over his paunch towards my offered light for his cigar. "For example, when I was stationed in Monterrey, I lived off base and rented a room out to

Aaron. That's how we met, sir."

"Please don't call me sir. I'm retired. You can call me Doc."

"I'm just a good ol' fashioned Southern boy," he said brokenly, sunburnt face glowing with each flaring puff. "Old habits die hard, Doctor Owen."

"Just Doc."

"Yes, Doc Owen," Cheek somewhat acquiesced with a grin.

"You were saying about the Navy?"

"Yes," Cheek said, blowing a cloud of white into the humid air. "When I was stationed in Monterrey I was able to live off base. Aaron rented a room from me. I much prefer living off base for reasons just like that. I wouldn't have met Aaron otherwise. That was, what, six years ago, Aaron?"

Aaron nodded, nearly sleeping in his rye.

"Didn't Aaron say you grew up out west?" Cheek asked Doc.

Doc smiled into his rye again, then answered, "I was the son of a West Texas minister. Very conservative upbringing, though as I got older and via the Army saw so much of the world, different issues began to take a higher priority for me. I used to be very Republican, for example, but have since found labels too confining."

"I understand, sir," Cheek said. "I'm from the Bible belt. Dad was a small-town miner. I define myself by those things, but that doesn't describe who I am or what I've seen or... what I've done."

The two veterans delved into a 'how the military

changed my life' conversation, and I drifted into my own thoughts. Specifically I pondered Doc's comment about having been Republican. It reminded me how they had occasionally hosted political events at their house and hired me to bartend. They paid me handsomely for a very simple job, no doubt figuring a college kid could always use some extra money. I had only known them a couple years at that point—having met Aaron only late in high school—and Aaron was far away, but they always treated me as an extension of their family.

And why not? Isn't that what family was all about? Sharing moments and helping each other out. I recalled the Canadian I rode with, or rather how Adrien had behaved. He delighted at every little moment of togetherness, every moment of shared humanity. He relished every surprise. I missed a great opportunity that day. Rather than enjoy the people, I had focused on their numbers. I felt overwhelmed and just wanted to get out. I begrudged those numbers because they made riding with Aaron impossible. Expectations dashed, I rode hard, leaving behind what RAGBRAI was all about. I rode alone.

But I wasn't alone. I'm not talking about the 15,000 members of RAGBRAI. I'm talking about 15,000 members of *family*. Expectation can be fun, but had a dangerous tendency to narrow awareness. I resolved to do better. Despite being exhausted, sleep came grudgingly, a suitable rebuke for my cowardice and impatience.

CHAPTER SEVEN

Twister Hill Confessions

The sky was dark when we rose. Our pre-biking rituals were performed quietly, partly due to fatigue that eight hour's rest had been unable to remedy, and partly because the ambiance demanded it. Far to the east, a strip of sunrise burned brilliant red. We pumped up tires by flashlight, silent, contemplative. Or were those just excuses to stall? Probably.

Aaron and I attached our usual bottle of Gatorade and one of water onto our bikes, then watched with amusement as Cheek wrestled with his poor, abused CamelBak. The holes had enlarged badly, torn during his struggles to remove the thing over sore, thick arms. Were it not for the sipping tube, the bladder would have fallen out entirely. Alas, we didn't have three bottles of the same Gatorade flavor left, so into the bladder he mixed up a bizarre cocktail of orange, watermelon, and some blue stuff called Glacier Freeze.

"So what's the plan for today?" I asked, munching on a fat cowboy cookie, provided with love by Aaron's mom Barbara. Such had been my secret weapon breakfast for the last two days.

"Haul ass," asserted Cheek.

"It's going to be longer than the last two days," Aaron said, squinting at the RAGBRAI guide with his flashlight. "But only 1,787 feet gain. That's less than half the hills from each of the previous days. But today's the second longest distance."

"How long?"

"Seventy-one miles," he said, nodding to the answering chorus of groans. "It's also going to be hotter today than before. Dad said yesterday's warnings were explicit about today being really bad."

"Home sweet home," I joked.

"Oh, I should tell, I should tell you I've heard there's a big hill at the end. They say it's huge."

"Twister Hill," Cheek said with a sharp, knowing nod.

"You've done it in the past?"

"No," he said. "Route's different every year. But I've talked to people who've done it. It'll be tough, but we're tough, too."

"I don't know how tough I'll be at the end of seventy miles cycling on the sun," Aaron said ominously.

We finally declared war on the road, and Cheek took off like a bullet. Aaron and I rode more or less quietly, soaking up the tranquility of early morning.

The air puffed fresh and damp, the clouds purred pinkish-red. Most riders respected the lingering, hushed atmosphere. The dominant sound was the soft whirring of gears. The hour was fairly small, so perhaps most people hadn't yet fully awakened. Certainly our bodies were slow to do so. After a while they expressed concern over such constant use. Concern we could handle. Rebellion was our worry. A general fatigue had settled into our bones, but our performance was buoyed by expectation of an easier day—barring the cringe-worthy end at Twister Hill, that is. That's where body rebellion threatened ambush.

In the first town we found Cheek easily. So small was Lidderdale that it took nearly all 186 residents to serve breakfast croissants and fruit at the fire station. Cheek hopped on the road, muffin in mouth, so that Aaron and I need not even slow down. The next town, Lanesboro, was even smaller at 121 folks. We skipped that, too, so focused were we. Amazingly, all three of us rode together all the way to the third blink-and-you'll-miss-it town of Churdan.

Though still early, the heat was rising. My companions mopped their brows almost continuously during the hard ride. A short break was in order. I opted for an Iowa tenderloin. It's hard to find a good fried tenderloin sandwich outside the Midwest.

The pork loin was so large that it had been tenderized and hammered out to double the length of the bun. Just right. Some people split such tenderloins in half to stack it double, whereas others get a second bun and make two sandwiches. That morning I chose the third option, which was to nibble the extending, exposed breaded tenderloin all around the bun. Standard was a healthy splat of yellow mustard and a couple slices of pickle. I never used to like mustard, but after befriending the king of a mustard empire in Romania, it was now my condiment of choice. See? Aaron's not the only one with stories.

"How can you eat that on such a hot, steamy morning?" asked Aaron. "It's so heavy."

Before I could answer, up came Cheek with a Styrofoam plate of pancakes, extra butter, extra syrup.

"Booster fuel for Twister Hill," Cheek said, hefting his pancakes.

We passed a peanut cart, which I couldn't resist. Nor could Cheek, of course. A hot-to-the-touch bag of steaming, cinnamon-coated almonds each and we were ready to go. Morning food report... *complete!*

Onward we rode, chewing up the miles. Rubber on concrete. Grease on calves. Sweat on crotch lube. The hours flew by until noon. We were on such a roll, in fact, that the boys somehow managed to convince me to pass Mr. Pork Chop without stopping. Tragic, I know. About 300 yards later, however, Aaron got our first flat tire.

"See?" I said. "It's a sign from the pork god. We've got to go back and have a Mr. Pork Chop."

"You already had a huge breaded tenderloin," Aaron pointed out.

I channeled Cheek by shrugging, but then added, "One cannot argue with divine intervention. Or should

I say porcine intervention?"

"And you say you write books?" Cheek said, incredulous. "Do people actually buy them?"

"Not so much," I replied Cheek-ishly.

"We might want to go back," Cheek said, ignoring my imitation. "The sun here is really rough. Lots of shade there."

The large cluster of trees did look invitingly close. The sun was directly overhead and beat down on us mercilessly. I glanced with concern to Aaron. His face had been in a permanent flush for three days, but was now looking positively wretched. Cheek's gray stubble glistened with sweat and the front of his T-shirt was dripping.

"You good at changing tires?" Cheek asked Aaron.

The Portlander removed his helmet to run a hand through his dripping hair. He shook his head. Sweat flung everywhere. "Never done it before. Can't be that hard."

"Are you kidding?" I asked, incredulous. "After all those years of biking...?"

"Portland," Aaron answered. "There's a bike shop on every corner."

"It's kinda tricky," I said. "I've only done it once, but that was in my garage."

"Bah," Cheek scoffed. "It's easy. Just do it."

Changing the tire proved to be fairly easy. Filling it with air was another matter. We had no pump, but rather the portable CO_2 cartridges for a fast fill. The problem was that his kit included a cartridge with threads, which necessitated fully tightening it onto the nozzle. It filled the tire just fine, but by the time he unscrewed it and wrestled it off the tire had deflated again.

We moved to my CO_2 kit, which had a trigger gun. My cartridge screwed safely into the mount, but pulling the trigger didn't release the gas. With all the care of handling a loaded revolver, we tried various tricks to get it to 'shoot'. No luck. Then the drama really began as we tried to get the failed cartridge back out of the gun. We were scared to unscrew it because the top was already punctured. Maybe it would shoot out or something. We passed the thing back and forth like a hot potato. It was not our finest moment.

After nearly twenty minutes of this, we were getting a little crazy from the heat. Aaron's face was so flushed he looked like he was going into heart failure. Finally Cheek grabbed the loaded gun and recklessly ripped off the cartridge. With a loud CRACK! the cartridge shot out like a bullet, flew right over my shoulder, and tore through the corn stalks. All three of us watched, aghast, as a shredded leaf swayed gently to the earth, blasted off its branch by the cartridge.

"Jesus, Cheek!" I cried.

"What?" he squawked. "You guys were being wimps, so I took care of it."

"Anybody got another cartridge?" Aaron asked, wiping his brow for the umpteenth time. Shrugs all around.

Fortunately we had oodles of help from passersby. We had waved off the first couple of dozen calls offering assistance, foolishly thinking we had things under control. People were amazingly kind and supportive. Those who didn't slow to offer aid at least called a friendly, "Stay cool!" or "Drink water!" The next person to offer assistance was taken advantage of. In fact, the man used his own CO_2 cartridge to show us what we were doing wrong. He had Aaron's tire perfect in seconds.

"You make it look easy," Aaron commented.

"Only took twenty years of flats to figure it out!" he replied as he remounted his bike.

"How much for the cartridge?"

"Don't worry about it," the Samaritan said. "I always bring a bunch of extras for things like this. Next town just buy an extra and pass it along to someone else in need."

Watching the man depart, Cheek commented, "I love Iowa."

"Don't try to suck up," I retorted. "You're still on my bad guy list."

"Ooh," Cheek replied in a mock fear.

To reward us for half an hour in the torrid heat, Aaron bought us smoothies at the next stop. A large, hilly yard before a tiny, century-old farmhouse was filled with perhaps a hundred relaxing riders. One of the more popular—and certainly most unique— vendors had set up there. We stared in wonder at a large contraption built of old Amana washers and dryers. It had been customized into an elaborate gearing of pistons and revolutions to create fresh ice cream. Unfortunately for them, however, the heat was so oppressive that things weren't working very well.

Though a time-tested vendor used to the hot July/August dog days, that year was literally the hottest of all 39 thus far. Buyers got wet, loose ice cream puddles they could lap up like cats. And many did just that.

Something else was in order for us, however. Cheek bought a round of ginger smoothies. "Delicious," he boasted as he handed them over. "And best of all: they settle stomachs."

"Some of us need that more than others," I jabbed.

Icy treats in hand, we moved into the shade offered by a thick grove of ancient, mighty oaks. Lying back on the luxuriantly thick grass, I slid my fingers in deeper. Below the wind-rustled yellow tips, down deep into the evergreen tangles near the roots, it was yet damp. The shy sensations tingled up my hand and tickled my wrist.

The simple pleasures of shade are so easily forgotten in our modernized lives. As adults we tend to focus on optimal comfort at every given moment. As a child, I remembered playing for hours in the snow without thought of temperature, let alone gloves or hats. Now my car's thermostat is measured by individual degrees Fahrenheit. As if we'd really notice the difference between 73 and 74°? Certainly in Las Vegas I couldn't tell the difference between 115 and 116! I fear we've gotten to the point where we react not to the actual weather, but to the quantified number that represents it. Moments like this reminded me that all you really need is a big ol' oak tree... and no thermometers, thank you. I suddenly better understood dogs, who, when finding a nice little spot of shade, whether in a doorway or under a bench, were content to nap therein. No, I still did not understand Cheek any better.

"Nice how we're all the same now," Aaron commented over resistant slurps of thick smoothie.

"The same?" Cheek asked, rather abrasively.

"The same, the same pace," Aaron was quick to clarify. "Hey, check out those penny farthings!"

He pointed to a cluster of old-style bicycles laboring by. Not just old-style, but *old*-style. That is, the 19th century high-wheel bicycles with a four-foot front wheel and a tiny little rear wheel, ridden by mustachioed gentlemen in brown bowler hats. In this case, however, the riders wore T-shirts.

"Gotta be day riders," Aaron said. "Imagine riding a single-gear penny farthing for a week."

"Or up Twister Hill," Cheek observed ominously.

Watching the high-wheels depart, I set my smoothie down. The strangest buzzing noise filled the air. We all stopped everything and automatically reached for cell phones.

"No bars," Aaron commented.

"No power," Cheek admitted. He hadn't remembered to charge his phone even once since arriving in Iowa. "Hey, what's that under your cup?"

Cheek motioned towards my cup with a nod. I grabbed the smoothie just as it began tumbling over. From beneath emerged a huge cicada, buzzing furiously. He didn't like the cold! Slowly he crawled atop the long grass to glare angrily at me.

"Even the bugs don't like you," Cheek noted.

Aaron, ever the peacemaker, advised sagely, "Best let sleeping cicadas lie."

Absently we watched the line of bicycles move on by. It was never-ending. We began to count the riders pointing out my green bike to companions. It was about all we had in us, considering the debilitating heat. That is, until two gorgeous young women saw big green. They swerved to get a closer look, motioning to their following friends to join them. Soon a whole gang of buxom beauties were zeroing in on the bike. They looked genuinely excited, though not nearly so much as Cheek.

"This is your big chance!" he exclaimed, smacking me on the arm with great force.

"*My* big chance?" I replied, taking pains to not rub my smarting arm. "I'm married. You go get 'em, tiger."

"It's my bike now!" Cheek cried as he thundered down the hill to accost the women.

"This ought to be good," Aaron noted.

But as the ladies neared the bike, their actions pantomimed obvious disappointment that it was just a cheap spray-paint job. Obvious contempt pinched their pretty faces. They waved the others off, shook their heads defiantly at the approaching, expectant Cheek, then returned to the road. Disappointment all around!

Cheek plopped back down beside us with a sigh. "Time to spill it. Why'd you paint your bike? You told the mechanic it was a moment of self-loathing."

A feigned angelic smile crept across his face as he

asked with faux innocence, "Tell us more about your self-loathing."

I snorted at the taunt, but acquiesced.

"The reason *was* prompted by disgust, but the actual idea came from a good place. I hate the bikers in Las Vegas. Every morning they'd prance around with their expensive bikes behind their expensive cars or, more likely, discuss their expensive gear while waiting in line for expensive coffee. That didn't bother me so much—to each his own—but on the road they were just as self-absorbed. Downright dangerous. I was nearly killed by a platoon of Lance wanna-bes who drove me off the road. That's not what biking should be, and I thought of Hans.

"Hans," I explained, "is a German guy I know who's literally biked the world: every continent but Antarctica. He rode across Africa twice, once east-west, once north-south. I saw a few of his slide shows, which were fascinating. Perhaps most amazing of all was that he rode alone: just him, his bike, and a tent out there for months. Amazingly, he never once got robbed. The trick he used to keep his bike from being stolen while sleeping on a roadside or in some stranger's house was to spray paint it really, really gaudily. Tires and everything. Poverty-stricken locals probably wouldn't care about how it looked, but it was imminently identifiable. I was inspired by the idea. Nobody in that part of Vegas would steal a lousy thousand-dollar bike, of course. It wasn't that. You see, Hans was contemptuous of image. He didn't have time for that: he was too busy crossing *yet another* continent—solo!

"So I got some spray paint. I wanted to paint it bright yellow, which is my favorite color, but I didn't want to seem like the Lance wanna-bes I was mocking: too much like the yellow Tour de France jerseys. But I wanted a color that was bold and bright and happy—"

"Which you are not," Cheek interrupted.

"—which I am not," I granted. "So Day-Glo green it was. When the time came to act upon my long-brewing emotions, I went a little nuts. I almost spray painted my helmet, the floor, the cats. I was giggling hysterically—crazy from the heat, maybe—and babbled out loud all the stupid jokes that came to mind. The Day-Glo green reminded me of bio-luminescence, so I began shouting bio-mechanical luminescence, then eventually just Brian-luminescence."

"Or Day-Glo Worm because you're so slow?" Cheek offered.

"You know what's the worst? The Green Lantern movie just came out, so everybody points and shouts 'look at the comic book loser!' I can't win."

"Not when I'm around," Cheek agreed.

"What about you," I said, amused by his barbs. "Since we're in the confessional, I gotta know why you're called Cheek."

"It's my call sign," he explained. "Once you get a name, you keep that crap forever. Early on in my career—after a real bender—I passed out in the shower. I was told my right butt cheek covered the drain, flooding the shower. When I woke up everybody called me Cheek. The first time I transferred to a new base, I tried to get out of it. When they asked my call sign I said with my best growl 'Ripper!', but within the day my real call sign was discovered. It's been following me for twenty years."

"How about you, Aaron?" I asked. "Any confessions?"

Aaron didn't miss a beat, answering, "None that I'm ready to admit in front of a writer!"

Someone, somewhere in the crowd, cranked up a weather report. We listened in, interested. We learned less about the heat and more about the community. Public radio is a great way to gauge what's important to local folks. In the case of the Midwest: *"Des Moines, Iowa, is experiencing its most prolonged heat wave in 20 years, according to Jim Keeney, a meteorologist with the Weather Service. The hot weather in the nation's breadbasket also poses a threat to farmers' top cash crop, corn, as it enters its key growth stage of pollination. The wet spring led to late planting of corn, and dry hot weather is adding concerns. 'Right now we are seeing real stress in the corn plants,' says Mark White, adviser to the Missouri Corn Growers Association."*

Cheek glanced around, earnest brow frowning in confusion. "If this is stressed corn," he observed, "I'd hate to see it happy. It's already ten feet tall."

"Oh, yes," Aaron said. "In Iowa, you can actually hear the corn grow."

Cheek raised an inquisitive brow.

"Plant the seed and stand back!" I joked. I thought I was funny—as usual—but worried I had somehow offended a nearby rider when he leaned in looking all serious. He was a remarkably fit, white-haired man in large, sweat-streaked glasses. He wore a baseball cap sporting a Con-Agra logo.

"I'm on the quest fer a 20-foot cornstalk this year," he said with much gravity. "Ain't no joke."

"Did you say *twenty* feet, sir?" Cheek asked, incredulously.

"That's right. Tough this year, though. Weather ain't cooperatin'. All this rain put off plantin' to the end o' April. Even then it was only 'bout 3% o' regular crop, statewide. Last year it was 'proximatee 67.2% by the same time."

"But only *approximately* 67.2%" Aaron muttered quietly, amused.

"Top tassel this year so far's 17 foot, 9 inches," the man continued, looking distressed. He all but spat out, "The Myers of Williamsburg."

"You don't say," Aaron encouraged whimsically.

"There's some test stalks on the corn cam," he continued. "Gotta 20-foot measurin' stick behind 'em. Even got the 17 foot, 9 inch mark of the Myers' stalk."

"We'll have to check it out, sir," Cheek said, even as the man launched into a lecture about the differences of hybridized versus heritage seeds in the quest for height. Cheek secretly motioned for us to make a break for it. That time all three of us tore up the next hill, eager to disappear.

As usual, Cheek soon pedaled away furiously into the horizon. This suited me just fine, for I finally had a chance to really talk to Aaron. I was hoping to talk about life, goals met or not, things like that. But Aaron really wanted to explain his experiences training.

"I'm sorry," he said, "But this heat is really getting to me. Seriously. It's just so different from what I've been training in. Portland has had record-setting rain and cold. It's been my experience that the rainy reputation of the Pacific Northwest isn't as bad as people think. But not 2011. That was *exactly* what everybody thinks. We had the second wettest spring since 1894, when they started keeping track. Washington had their wettest. When the weather forecast said 'chance of rain' or even 'partly cloudy', that meant rain all day. It rained every single day in March. And it was cold rain, too. In fact, I remember by Memorial Day we had had a record of 229 days without three consecutive days reaching just seventy degrees."

"I remember the day it got to me," Aaron added thoughtfully. "I mean, we're all used to cloudy and rainy. But on one of my longer training rides I was huddling under an overpass, trying to stay warm. I decided to check my voicemails. I opened the coat pocket and rainwater sheeted off my shoulders right into the pocket. Filled it. Flooded the phone and left me with an Apple brick—the iBrick, I suppose. With numb fingers I pulled out a Clif Bar, but was so sick of them, and so cold, I rode straight to the nearest place, an IKEA store. I stamped through all muddy and got some potatoes and meatballs and anything else that was hot."

I hadn't thought about his issues, I admitted to

myself. They were so alien to me! But really, the thought of something to eat during a ride—*anything* other than a melted energy bar or puddle of Gu-Chomps... *in shade*, no less—sounded like luxury. I paused in reflection, then started laughing.

"What?" Aaron asked, smiling encouragingly at my mirth.

"I just remembered an email you once sent," I said. "Your 'nightmare training story' was basically you waiting out the rain while being 'forced' to eat empanadas from a street vendor in a beautiful city park."

"It was, it was most trying," he laughed. "To my waistline, anyway."

"Not to steal your thunder, but let me tell you about a *truly* horrific training ride...

"I had to wake up at 2:30 in the morning to beat the heat. After an hour drive I was at mile marker 0 in the desert north of Las Vegas. The sun didn't rise for an hour more, so I had to ride by flashlight for the first hour. That part of the ride was quite nice, actually. There was even life. I mean, they haven't dropped a nuclear bomb there in forty years, right? I saw a coyote and even a desert fox. At mile marker 33—which I remember very clearly, mile marker 33—I saw a huge jack rabbit dead on the road. Its guts were spread everywhere, ravens circling above. The whole 'death in the desert' thing. I rode on and had the usual struggles riding through the Muddy Mountains.

"Strange name, that," I added thoughtfully. "Because mud implies moisture. There's absolutely none, of course. They're just so damn ugly that they look like a giant pile of solidified mud. That's the complimentary description. It really looks like the mound of brown you'll see looking into a pit latrine. Anyway, that was the good part of the ride, so I won't complain about it."

"A rarity," Aaron noted.

"To be sure," I agreed. "So, on my return I had to pass mile marker 33 again and the dead rabbit. By then it was late morning and the ravens had hours to rip the carcass apart. They were still dancing their happy dead-animal dance on the road when I approached. They flew off, but one tried to take lunch with him. He grabbed a huge, dripping piece of intestine or whatever and flapped off with it. It was three feet long and obviously too heavy. Can you believe he dropped it on me?"

My stomach roiled at the recollection.

"So there I was, covered in steaming entrails in 110 degree heat, with two more hours of panting to go. It hit *130* in that time. No shade, of course, except the port-a-potty set up for some construction guys, who were nowhere to be found. Probably at a nearby brothel called the Shady Lady. Out there, *any* reference to shade—pun or not—would lure *any*one. Even a nun. So I spent a quick break in the dubious shade of a port-a-potty that was baking in the sun. Can you possibly imagine how happy the flies were with me? Sunblock, sweat, poop and guts... I was a freakin' buffet!"

"Another *Comedy of Errors*," Aaron said with a

chuckle. "Perhaps this explains why you're such a sourpuss."

"No, that would be my ex-wife," I quipped.

Soon we passed Cheek recovering at the side of the road. He was sitting on a folding chair beside a large vendor truck. Aaron and I pulled over to regard the man, for he was exhibiting most unusual behavior. For Cheek, that's saying a lot. His chair sat directly in the blazing hot sun—all but for his head, which remained in the angle of shade. All evidence pointed to his having been there awhile, probably having chosen the spot when it was fully shaded. But that had obviously been an hour ago. Had he been asleep, we would have understood. But he wasn't asleep. He was staring at nothing, like a propped up corpse.

"Cheek!" Aaron called. "What are you doing in the sun?"

The sailor grunted, but did not otherwise stir.

"Cheek!"

"Mmph."

Finally his eyes focused. He looked about, disoriented.

"You're in the sun," Aaron said, helpfully explaining the obvious.

Cheek tried to move, but was unable to do so. Once he sat down, his joints had locked up. The sun crept over his body inch by inch, yet he had been unable to avoid it. He was a wreck. With a lot of grunting and swearing and horrendous cracking of joints, we managed to pull him up and move him into what little shade the truck offered.

"Don't think I been hydrating enough," he croaked as we put an icy, sweating bottle of Gatorade in his gloved hand.

"You have a CamelBak half-full of Gatorade," Aaron pointed out.

"Forgot," he mumbled.

But then he suddenly perked up and pushed himself to his feet with a tremendous surge. We watched as he stomped around the vendor truck and ordered them to top off his CamelBak with ice water. Out of ice water, they admitted. Gatorade, he said. Just gave you the last, they said. Whatcha got that's cold? Ice coffee. So Cheek topped off his CamelBak with iced coffee... on top of three different Gatorade flavors. Every sip brought a wince.

"We gonna kick Twister Hill's ass, or what?" Cheek boomed, even as he pedaled off into the summer sun. We didn't let him get away with it this time, however. We were concerned enough to muscle up to him. By pure luck, that happened to be just another mile or two away, in the town of Paton.

Paton was the hometown not only of the fictional Private Ryan—played by Matt Damon in the movie— but also real-life astronaut Loren Shriver. He was not present because he was also riding RAGBRAI. Still, the locals made sure there was plenty of freeze-dried ice cream in his honor.

"I need air conditioning," Aaron declared, though I sensed it was a ruse to get Cheek better recovered. Well, not entirely. The cumulative effect of the record-breaking heat over all those hills and miles was extremely debilitating on both of them. We wandered the tiny, tiny town of Paton until we found an old-style diner. Inside were half a dozen stools at the counter, several tables of portable food, and throughout all was glorious air conditioning.

While we rested in the relative coolness—with so many bodies packed within, the AC struggled to compensate—I was intrigued by their advertisements for walking tacos. I ordered one and was handed a single-serving bag of Nacho Cheese Doritos that had been packed with additional seasoned ground beef and onions. After being topped with shredded cheese and lettuce, they stuck a fork in it and called it a walking taco. Though a taco snob—an everything snob, really, who am I kidding?—I had to admit it was quite tasty. Perhaps even borderline genius.

Eventually Cheek led us into the smallest grocery store I had ever seen. A 7-Eleven was a mall by comparison, for this dinky, one-room structure was smaller than my living room. It took all of seconds to see they did not offer the jar of pickles Cheek desired. He stepped up to the counter to inquire.

"Good afternoon, ma'am," he said respectfully to the slender, fifty-something woman with curly hair and big glasses. "Do you sell pickles?"

"No, I'm sorry," she replied. "I'm sure you can find them in Pilot Mound…"

She trailed the sentence somewhat oddly, prompting Cheek to inquire, "Are you sure?"

"Well, no," she admitted, looking a bit put off by the question. "I've never been there."

"You new to the area, then?"

"Me?" she asked, obviously surprised at his conclusion. "Oh, no. I've lived here my whole life."

Pilot Mound was only ten miles down the road.

Pilot Mound, like all towns that day, was small. Strange, then, to see the giant People's Saving Bank. This huge, gorgeous brick two-story structure knocked our socks off. Perhaps my favorite thing about RAGBRAI thus far was the exposure to so much amazing architecture from the mid-late 1800s. It was a different era, a time when the expanding frontier was hacked out by hardy men and women, the townships peopled by bold entrepreneurs, men of vision who jockeyed for county seats or, far more lucratively, access to the burgeoning trans-continental railroad. The bank was a masterpiece of that era, and equally dead. The bones of a once-mighty beast rising from the dust, sad and lonely and forgotten. The dirt-caked windows had surely not been cleaned since WWII. They wore no protective boards, for who would vandalize in a town such as this? Barely half a dozen structures lived in the present, each small and humbled by the dominating monument to a hopeful past.

Cheek all but fell into someone's backyard to lay down in the shade, Aaron stumbling along after. Both lie down next to each other, arms laid across chests in repose, like two fallen warriors. The only sign they yet lived was a gentle groan that escaped Aaron's parted lips. As Cheek drifted off, I barely heard him mutter,

"Sorry, Brian. Sucks to be you." The words were so quiet, I wondered if I had imagined them. The admission was surely unconscious.

While they napped I wandered the town. I wanted to give them plenty of time to rest up before the day's toughest challenge. Twister Hill lurked nearby. Its dread name was born of the filming here of several scenes in the blockbuster movie *Twister*. The beast lay between us and our final destination. The hush that accompanied its very mention was a testament to the fear the hill evoked. It might as well have been the dragon rather than the Lonely Mountain from *The Hobbit*.

I worried for my companions, seeing how they were really, really hurting from the heat. They weren't alone. Everywhere I looked were men and women collapsed in the shade, shaking their heads in wonder. Most were too tired and too hot to speak intelligibly. Mumbles about Twister Hill droned low through the hot air, like an agitated but smoked beehive. When I returned, Cheek was gone. No surprise there. A few minutes later Aaron woke up. Though smiling ruefully, he gamely said, "Let's do this."

After Pilot Mound, the road dropped into the forested valley of the Des Moines River. At the bottom, the bridge was not particularly big, nor the river particularly wide, but—like my ex-wife—its abrasiveness belied its size. Beyond, the road sloped upward, ever upward, rising out of the valley straight and true as an arrow shot into the sun.

The road-side scenario on that climb began to

confuse me. Copious riders left the road to huddle under the nearby trees as if it were raining. At first I thought there was a popular vendor hiding in the recessed forest. Considering the oddly vacant faces, I suspected a beer tent. Everyone panted with sawing, gasping breaths like fish out of water. Even their eyes bulged grotesquely as they glanced about. No, those weren't signs of inebriation, but looks of shock, of horror, of hurt.

On the sunny road itself, cyclists flowed to the side and slowed to a crawl, bikes wobbling, struggling to stay upright. Soon I was forced to weave around and through the retreating riders in an effort to keep my momentum going.

"What the Hell...?" I muttered as yet another cyclist before me all but exploded and flared down and out, billowing smoke. I swerved, sped up, slowed down, ducked and surged. Climbing the hill became chaotic as an aerial dogfight: the Battle of Britain, the assault on the Death Star—choose your metaphor. About halfway out of the valley, I realized what was going on. Twister Hill!

The hill was long indeed, and steep, but not as long and steep as I had envisioned. Straight up it stretched, ever longer, only at the very top did it curve and disappear into the surrounding forest. But compared to the 5-mile ascents up rocky, sun-seared desert mountains I had trained on, this was short and sweet. I was not cocky about it—a real rarity, to be sure —because I well knew that we all had our own challenges. Measuring up to ourselves was all that mattered. And my thighs burned pleasantly from the exertion.

At the top were several dozen people sprawled upon the grass in the shade or, at best, leaning heavily upon their bikes, panting. Directly before me a rider of perhaps retirement age collapsed. Bike, gear, and all slammed to the pavement to clatter roughly over the road. I swerved and loosed a cry of warning, even as bystanders rushed to retrieve the fallen warrior from the battle zone. The hapless man was pulled into the shade—still with a heat-index over 110°—and the good folks of RAGBRAI took care of him like pros. In a blink he was holding a bottle of ice water in one hand and a banana in the other, while the crowd stayed back to give him room to breathe. A kindly lady fanned him with a magazine.

Oh, and Aaron nearly died.

The man from Portland refused to be defeated. Slow and steady he pushed up the long, steep, heated slope. At the very top he slowed to almost a standstill. His bike wavered dangerously, and I thought for sure he was going to collapse. But with brow set firmly, he determinately pressed harder and harder, on and on. Slowly, agonizingly slowly, the rhythmic force moved him, inch by inch, over the brow of the hill. He passed right by where I waited, never once looking at me, at the forest, at anything but the concrete beneath his tires. And onward he went, beyond my sight and around the bend.

A mile later I caught up to where Aaron came to rest. He couldn't have found a more inviting place: a small, single-story farmhouse whose cropland had been rented out. A retired couple had lovingly crafted a paradise of numerous gardens and copious flowers, complete with shrub-lined pools and fountains. Watermelon in hand, Aaron stumbled through the paradise, looking for a free spot. He gravitated towards a lush hedge of ten-foot lilac bushes. Amazingly, we found Cheek there. He was fast asleep, beefy arm draped over his face. Two slabs of watermelon lay destroyed beside him.

Aaron plopped down into the soft grass beside Cheek and tore into his watermelon.

"Sorry I passed you by," he finally said over a mouthful of melon. "But I had to keep going. If I stopped, I don't think I could have gotten up again."

"I think you did great!"

"Let me guess," he said ruefully. "You never lowered out of top gear?"

"Actually, I dropped from 24 all the way down to 21," I admitted.

"You da man," Aaron said. His simultaneous spitting out a watermelon seed revealed how he really felt.

I struck a weightlifter's pose but, after a disparaging remark from a passerby, sheepishly dropped it. When I turned back to Aaron, he had passed out cold. So rapid had been the onset of sleep, he hadn't even set aside his watermelon. With a smile I regarded my companions as they literally snored in the peaceful garden, cheeks glistening with watermelon juice and seeds even stuck to their whiskers.

CHAPTER EIGHT

Children of the Corn

Surprisingly, the high-water mark of drama on Day 3 was not Twister Hill. No, that was not nearly as trying as what occurred *after* arriving at our final destination. We couldn't find the camp. The lack of clear signs was distressing, and Cheek was maddening. The man, clearly at the end of his endurance, stopped *five* times in the first mile of town. He stalled more and more as we pushed deeper and deeper into the tree-lined, hilly streets of Boone. Twilight shadows tumbled over lawns, then curbs, then finally us.

"This isn't working," I muttered after our umpteenth pause.

"What's up with this town?" Aaron grumbled irritably. "The only signs I've seen are proclamations that Boone is the home of Pufferbilly Days. Is there a useful sign anywhere in this town?"

"Awhile back was a sign for Boone Valley Brewing," Cheek pointed out. "If we wait there, think Doc will come looking for us?"

Without waiting for an answer, he began pulling off the road yet again. Aaron cajoled him to keep moving.

"Maybe, maybe I can get reception at the top of this next hill," Aaron suggested.

Cheek's groan at the indicated ascent made the extra effort a joy—for me, anyway. Finally we stopped, exhausted, at the top of the huge, tree-shaggy hill. We listened for tell-tale sounds of RAGBRAI revelry, hoping for a clue to our destination, but heard only crickets. Beneath the surrounding oaks, all was dark and still. Ancient tombstones blurred with night-shrouded trunks, for the forest had long ago crept in, nibbling at the moldering graveyard more and more, decade after decade.

"I love old cemeteries!" Cheek boomed, dumping his bike on the curb. He marched off into the cemetery, calling, "Let's read the inscriptions."

His real motivation was soon revealed, however, for seconds later he was propped against an oak, eyes closed.

"Oh no you don't!" I called. "We're obviously close to being done. Let's just figure it out so we can really rest for the night."

"I'll bet this is a pioneer cemetery," Aaron mused. "I wouldn't be adverse to reading a few tombstones."

"You're not helping," I whined. "It's been a really long and hot day. You sure you want to drag it out any more?"

Checking for cell signal, Aaron and I circled the crown of the hill. Nothing. We rode over to another, then still another. Cheek we left with the dead. We were about to search for a pay phone when Aaron finally received a text from Doc. His directions indicated we were only about a mile and a half away.

"Oh," said Aaron. "The name of this park is McHose. Insert joke here. I'm too tired to make one of my own."

We shook Cheek awake and told him the news. "Great!" he cried. "Can I use the restroom first?"

Before we could answer, he walked across the street to disappear into another section of the large park. It was a long walk, but he tellingly refused to bike the distance. Aaron and I were forced to wait another twenty frustrating minutes.

"*Comedy of Errors*," Aaron said with amused—if dwindling—patience.

The parking lot of the Des Moines Area Community College had been appropriated for the RVs. Appropriated was too light a term to describe the situation—more like invaded. Squeegeed into every square foot of asphalt was a metal beast, generator growling, slamming doors barking. They fit so tightly into the lot, mismatched facing this way and that, intertwined, it was a wonder they got in at all. It was like some evil game of Tetris. Perhaps most amazingly of all, however, was that Doc's RV was right up front and center.

After 70+ miles in 110+ degrees, a shower was

most necessary. Alas, the RV had run low on water. But RAGBRAI always provides. Boone provided access to the college's locker room for five bucks. High schools were frequently opened to cyclists, as were public pools. That first night, in Glendale, I had showered at the junior high school. I had felt rather odd being in a boy's-only area as an adult, a *naked* adult, that is. But feelings of being a creep melted away in the cold blast of clean water. And that had been *before* the ride started. Now, after a full day of biking across summer Iowa, sweat-soaked and hosting more dead bugs than a windshield, I would have gladly subjected myself to a carwash.

In fact, a carwash was available. That was so much more interesting than, say, a towel sticking out of a mailbox to indicate a local willing to let riders use their shower. Not that I was dismissing such generosity, but famed were the RAGBRAI 'carwashowers'. While they varied from town to town, it was not uncommon to find a professional car wash that had installed shower heads, put up a few curtains, and even changed the chemicals... slightly. On the selector knob the de-greaser is still present and heavily partaken of, but they add deodorant soap and, for the final rinse, insect repellant!

By the time I tiptoed back through the college, past the hordes of riders filling the hallways as if it were lunchtime on a school day, Cheek and Aaron had already fallen asleep. It was not yet 8PM. Doc and I sat outside enjoying our respective routines, he sipping Templeton Rye, me smoking a maduro belicoso.

"Did you have any trouble finding the RV parking?" I asked Doc. "For riders, the signs were severely lacking."

"Not at all," Doc answered. "My experience has been that RAGBRAI is exceptionally well organized. The producers put together special maps for team drivers showing us the easiest way to get to the next town along alternate routes, since the route itself is closed to auto traffic. There's a lot of us, too. Doesn't matter what's driven—RV, school bus, van, whatever—someone needs to bring all the gear from point A to point B. Of course solo riders can pay the Des Moines Register's semi to haul their bags, but good luck finding them."

"Well, you certainly found a good spot today. You got here before the crush, then?"

"I make a habit of leaving as soon as you guys do, even predawn sometimes. That's how I always get the best spot at the next town. I set up the RV, the awning, the grill, whatever. I'll take stock of services you might need, such as finding where the showers are for you guys today. Then I settle in with my Kindle. I read in the shade, eat more cookies than I let Barbara know, and wait for you guys."

"Reading one of my books?"

"Um..." Doc hummed, stalling. Finally he just moved on, saying, "It's been a very relaxing week for me. No drama is a good thing."

I snorted in agreement.

"Well, Junior overcame all drama today admirably," I offered. With a sudden frown, I added,

"But he's not actually a junior, is he? He's Aaron Matthew Owen, but you're Aaron Randall Owen II, right? You call him Aaron anyway, so why not make him a full 'third'? That way I could call him 'Tree'. That'd be fun."

"Jr's and III's have their place of pride in family, but so frequently it's a matter of ego for the father," Doc answered. With an amiable smile he quickly added, "Not that I don't have an ego. But I had hopes for his individuality."

I nodded and loosed a puff of cigar smoke. The fumes lazed nearby in the hot air, as if unable to penetrate the dense humidity. Instead the cloud remained strangely intact, gently pulsing and rotating overhead. I liked Doc's reasoning and thought it a nice reminder that people should perhaps actually think things through before acting. Wonder what the world would be like if we all did that? Better, for sure. But probably a bit boring.

"You know," Doc added quietly, "I really appreciate how you all are treating me as 'one of the guys'."

"You are," I said simply.

"Not exactly. I was really concerned about being intrusive. This is Aaron's vacation, and I wanted him to have a week as relaxed as possible. Relatively speaking. But I am his father, after all."

"You've yet to spank him for being bad."

"He has Isabel for that now," Doc said with a smile.

"Once grown up, didn't you hang out with your

father as 'one of the guys?'" I asked.

A wry smile teased Doc's lips.

"Not exactly," he replied. "My father was a West Texas minister who never laughed in his life. I recall a classmate of mine from Spur..."

"Wait a minute," I interrupted. "You're from *Spur*, Texas? You just made that up."

"Nope, it's true," Doc replied. "Our high school class numbered about two dozen. It was so small that I not only played on the football team, but had to march in the band during halftime. As I was saying, I had a classmate named Priscilla, whose father had a big ranch that hosted the original rattlesnake rodeo. Yes, really. At that time it was open only to members of the Texas Peace Officers Association, the Texas Rangers, and I believe the Highway Patrol. My father was always invited through church connections to offer the invocation for the event. I wish I could remember exactly how he worded the blessing for an event that was centered around displays of personal firepower and the shooting of rattlesnakes in various venues. So no, my father was never 'one of the guys'. Certainly not in any sense that I cared to be a part of."

"Well this week you're just one of the guys," I reassured. "Unarmed, true, and a little balder, but also a lot smarter."

"No, just more experienced. But you're right about being balder."

An hour later I, too, was ready to retire. After a yawn and a stretch, I leaned conspiratorially to Doc and asked, "Any chance you could set the alarm to

5:00 instead of 5:15? We'd be done with the shortest day that much sooner, and no one would notice."

Doc smirked and revealed, "I've already done that two days in a row."

That night I slept in the RV because there was no room to set up the tent outside. I certainly wasn't going to lay my sleeping bag out beneath a dozen rumbling RV air conditioners. Concern of overcrowding was half the reason I hadn't slept in the RV yet, but I happily discovered how silly that was. Both Cheek and I slept on full-sized cots laid perpendicularly to the length of the vehicle, along with an aisle *and* a couch! It was glorious inside, but very cold to me. I was unused to 'normal people temps', so I slept under extra blankets and even a few stacked pillows. Beside me, however, Cheek lay passed out on top of the sheets in his underwear.

I listened to Cheek snoring loudly. Would he be able to handle this week? I wondered how I would handle it if this... I can't say *uninvited* guest... made us fail. Optimistic talk with Aaron's father aside, we all knew Aaron and Cheek weren't doing well. I was right to be worried. On Day 4, the Tire Dips failed.

I awoke, nose plugged up solid. Can't win for losin', as they say!

Our tire-pumping ritual proceeded quietly through a dew-heavy, cloudy predawn. We could tell the day was going to be very, very muggy.

"'Clouds, short, and flat' will be our motto today," Aaron said, noting it was the shortest day of the weeklong ride. Not just shortest, at a mere 55 miles, but easiest, with only 1200 feet of elevation gain. The guys could use it, too. Twister Hill had nearly broken them. Aaron continued reading from his iPhone, *"Significant relief from the heat is not anticipated through at least Saturday... increased chances of thunderstorm."*

"What?" I squawked. "Did you say rain? You mean, like, *riding* in the rain? The sky is falling! The sky is falling!"

"His true colors emerge," Cheek observed. His victory was lessened a bit by his mumbling the words with a mouth full of cowboy cookie.

We decided to skip sightseeing and hammer out Day 4 so as to just sit on our butts, rather than our saddles. Today was the day for all good things to come together. We were going to kick serious pedal. Because it was flat, because it was short. There was no sun, there was no wind. No, *we* were the wind! By the time we three hit the second town, half the ride was done and it was still very early morning.

Slater offered food vendors galore, including a whole bunch we had not yet seen, including Mexican. It was very crowded, the main street a thick throng of bodies swilling beer and snarfing breakfast burritos under a heavy sky. The temptation was too much for Cheek, and he disappeared. Aaron and I let him go, preferring to wander a few blocks through some stately ivy-shrouded buildings. A corner office had the rather amusing sign that read, *'Good Grief, Inc. End-of-Life Services.'* Behind the tall building of cherry-red brick was a lush garden. As foodies, we were thusly garden lovers. The green onions were so prolific as to actually push through the cracks in the brick walk and the wooden borders like weeds!

Overall, our stay in Slater was brief. We were all business, Aaron and I, and abandoned our search for Cheek in favor of chugging through the muggy miles. Aaron seemed fully recovered from the previous day's taxing ride. The rain seemed scared to fall. Hours flashed by, as did towns: Sheldahl, Alleman, White Oak, Elkhart. Finally a break seemed in order. We paused on a roadside to buy slices of watermelon from the back of a farmer's truck. He had filled the entire bed of his Ford with ice water, in which bobbed whole watermelons and jugs of milk. We munched on the almost too cold fruit and spit seeds out over a barbed wire fence. Directly opposite us, beyond a shrub-choked creek, two dairy cows munched placidly.

"Please tell me those are cows," I said offhandedly to Aaron.

He looked up from his iPhone with surprise. With confusion he noted the large, spotted, and obviously bovine animals.

"Just making sure it wasn't a mirror," I explained. "I think I'm gaining weight on this trip."

"Heat indices for yesterday reached 129° in Newton," Aaron said, wisely ignoring me and returning to his far more engaging iPhone. "According to the National Weather Service, twenty-two people already died from the heat and humidity."

Only half hearing him, I kept staring at the cows, muttering, "I wonder how they're handling the heat."

"Not well," Aaron answered. "They died."

"No, I mean the cows. I don't know much about cows, but I know if they die of heat they'll explode."

After a long pause, Aaron finally said, "I'm really not sure what Aurelia saw in you. She wasn't some sort of Romanian mail-order bride stuck with the highest bidder, was she?"

"Really," I pressed. "You know that, right? People do, too. Human bodies bloat in the sun just like cow bodies, due to expanding gasses like methane. If there's no release, through some orifice or another, it explodes. Such is life."

"Such is death," Aaron corrected.

Alas, 4000 cattle *did* die in Iowa alone that heat wave, according to the Iowa Cattlemen's Association. Despite having 1.2 million cattle—the fifth largest cattle-producing state in the nation—cattle are utterly unsuited to life in Iowa. Compare Daisy, the modern milk cow, to what nature selected for this environment: the buffalo. Their shaggy coats shrugged off the sun as easily as a blizzard, and were too thick for mosquitoes to puncture. Further, lots of cows were bitten by bats. I pity anyone trying to nibble on a live buffalo.

But the buffalo were long gone. At risk now was perhaps the last of Iowa's most prolific game. The pheasant, once king of Iowa's nearly half-a-billion-dollar hunting industry, was vanishing from the state. The population in 2012 was the second lowest on record, a whopping 81% below the average over the past *four decades*. For those disinterested in the ecological implications of this, the economic numbers were equally terrorizing. Iowa used to average 50,000 out-of-state pheasant hunters every year; men and women spending money in hotels, motels, diners, and shops. In 2010 that number was an income-killing low of 8,800.

To me it looked like there was a lot of untrammeled land, but that was surely just the cynic in me surprised it wasn't all gone already. I knew full-well that Iowa's cash cow was corn—a strangely worded statement, to be sure. Rising commodity and land prices—not to mention America's addiction to corn syrup—were overcoming appreciation for wildlife habitat and hunting inheritance. Only 1.5% of Iowa's natural habitat was public, which meant a whole lot of farmers with a whole lot of incentive to slash and grow. The downsides of this short-sighted, if understandable, behavior reached far and wide, from increasing soil erosion to contaminated water tables to the wholesale destruction of Iowa's once-mighty pheasant hunting tradition.

Keeping our morbid thoughts aloft, we soon passed a dead raccoon. It had been struck by a car and lie in the center of the road. Mercifully it remained whole, looking as peaceful as a cat napping on a sunny kitchen floor. This helped ease my sorrow at seeing such a charismatic animal slain so carelessly by man. Slain, but not ignored: for Team Roadkill staked their claim. Before our very eyes, a cluster of riders stopped to bestow upon the carcass a wreath of Mardi Gras beads.

"All this death in the cornfields is freakin' me out," I said. "It's like *Children of the Corn* or something. Can we just talk about—I don't know— maybe football?"

"The Iowa Hawkeyes fell from ninth overall rank to drop entirely off the charts," Aaron replied. With a sudden smirk, he added, "I think I'm getting the hang of your morbidity. It's fun for a change."

Onward we flew, for more miles meant more surprises. Rueful thoughts aside, things were going splendidly. The morning had been cloudy and almost cool—by comparison to the previous days, anyway. We were almost done with the entire ride and it was barely noon. Cheek was not present. So delighted was I that I made the most foolish of mortal mistakes: I stated aloud how well things were going.

WHAM!

The sun blasted apart the clouds to hammer down on us. It flashed Vegas-hot, as if to make up for time lost in the morning. Humidity gelled the air too thick to breathe. It felt like we had been immersed in a giant cauldron of hot maple syrup.

BAM!

Aaron's back tire exploded. Spokes popped like popcorn and suddenly the entire rim wanged into a weird, torqued shape that refused to spin at all. The wheel locked up with instant rigor mortis. Aaron almost collapsed into the grass-choked ditch.

"This is bad," Aaron said, frowning down at his defeated, brutalized bike. I snorted at the understatement.

"Time for a powwow," he said. Together we leaned over his iPhone to check our position.

"According to the handy-dandy RAGBRAI app, we're about five and a half miles from Bondurant," he said. "Last town was about two miles back."

We squinted into the heat-wavering horizon, loathe to backtrack two full miles.

"I can't recall if they had a repair tent," I ventured. "That would be a bitch of a retreat if it were for nothing."

Aaron nodded slowly. He was deep in thought, so I remained quiet. Yes, it was difficult.

"I love my wife," Aaron said suddenly, "but that doesn't mean I want her to win."

"What's that supposed to mean?"

"Isabel bet me a hundred bucks that I couldn't do it," he explained. "RAGBRAI."

"Behind every great man is a great woman supporting him," I teased.

"All week I've been dreaming about what I'd spend the money on," Aaron continued. "Day 1 it was all meat, maybe some high-quality Iowa beef I'd bring home as spoils of war. Day 2 it was all fresh vegetables from the farmer's market back in Portland. Day 3 it was booze, of course."

"Now we're talking," I approved.

We were stalling, and we knew it. Neither of us wanted to say the dread word. Aaron finally found the courage to speak it... in a roundabout way, of course.

"It all started when my marathon plans went awry," he began slowly. "Like a good caveman wannabe, I bought a pair of five-finger running shoes. I wanted to tap my inner ancestor, but couldn't run barefoot on concrete. This seemed the closest I could get, though in retrospect they were probably a bit too small. I ended up injuring my right foot. After a few months of therapy, RAGBRAI came up as a less painful alternative to running. But after watching me walk away from the marathon, Isabel was skeptical I could jump from a failed 26 miles to 500. So she bet me $100 I wouldn't finish with a mocking—but loving— deal."

"It's not the money," he finished. "It's the principle. I'll be damned if I lose. I won't use the sag wagon."

There. He said it. *Sag wagon.* A ripple of dread made me shiver, despite the heat. The sag wagon was the support vehicle nobody wanted to encounter. While it hauled spare parts and maybe luggage from time to time, its real purpose was to haul broken bikes and broken riders. It meant rescue. It meant failure. Aaron looked at me, deadly serious, and said, "I'm walking."

"What?" I said, surprised.

"If I walk the distance to Bondurant, I can still count it legally. Isabel's going down."

Too surprised to answer intelligently, I fell back on what usually works, saying, "May I insert a dirty joke?"

"You may not."

"That sounds a bit premature," I continued, then wistfully asked, "Can that even still happen at our age?"

"I'll let Cheek answer that," Aaron replied. He forced a grin, but we both knew our attempts at lightening the mood were poor.

"All right, then," I said, finally resolved to quit stalling. "Let's do it."

"Oh, no," Aaron said. "I don't want to hold you back. It's your vacation, too."

"Are you kidding? I'm only here to be with you. So let's do it. Do you think you can coast down this hill? It looks to be at least half a mile down."

"I don't think so," Aaron said, shaking his head. "I think the rim would collapse under my weight. For sure I'd have to remove the back brake so the wobbly rim will fit. That size hill with only a front brake is a game I don't want to play."

So onward we walked into the new, hot universe after that sudden, unwelcome big bang. For approximately ten billion years we walked. The universe was surely expanding. How else to explain why our destination remained ever out of reach? Surely it was moving at a much greater pace than our heat-sore feet.

For the first mile the ditch dropped down right beside the road, so we had to march extra carefully to avoid a tumble. That narrow strip of gravel was all we knew. Yet hope beckoned from afar. We excitedly pointed out a water tower not too far ahead. Checking for water towers was something all RAGBRAI riders did subconsciously. It was oh so reassuring to see the tell-tale sign of an oasis. But as we continued, the road curved away. The water tower was not that of Bondurant, but some other town.

Disappointment exploded within us, hot as the birth of our sun. Another four billion years passed. Was the present upon us? We were too sun-struck to think. Slowly, oh so slowly, we trudged up yet another hill. Atop it rested a large farmhouse offering merciful shade. There rested several dozen riders beneath a copse of old, gnarled oak trees. Still more riders swamped a vendor selling Hawaiian shaved ice.

"I need some shade," Aaron said, dropping his bike. It clattered to the gravel, voicing disdain at such abuse.

He pulled off his helmet to drag an arm across his glistening forehead. His hair was sloppy as a mop pulled from a bucket of sweat. Worse, his face was beet-red. His Pacific Northwest skin had literally not been in the sun for months, and now flared a fiery red even despite thick sunblock.

"Um..." I began tentatively.

"Yeah," he said. "Money or not, I can't walk in this sun. My skin can't handle it at this slow pace. I'm going to wait here for the sag wagon. You go on ahead."

"I'll wait for you in Bondurant," I offered.

"No, the overnight stop is only about seven miles from here," he replied. "You could be there in no time. There's no reason for you to waste your afternoon waiting in Bondurant when the finish is only a few miles further. Seriously."

"All right," I said, recognizing how much it pained him to be holding back a friend. "I'll wait in Bondurant about forty-five minutes or so. If we can't meet up there, I'll head to the RV. It's still really early, so it's no big deal. Besides, I'm sure Bondurant is so rockin'-awesome I won't want to leave."

Bondurant was not so rockin'-awesome I didn't want to leave. There was nothing wrong with it, of course, but it was very quaint. I liked it, actually. I watched riders sign a six-foot mini silo with their name and place of origin. I dutifully signed Aurelia's name and then checked my email at the local library, which was kindly opened to riders. Then I spied the mech tent, right across the street from the library and prominent with lots of spare parts. I found a shaded spot nearby and prepared for a wait.

To my surprise, the sag wagon approached just five minutes later. Said vehicle was a large van hauling a trailer of dead bikes. The van was black and foreboding, like a pestilence wagon hauling victims out of a medieval city. But its approach meant success for us. If Aaron only needed to ride a few miles, how could Isabel consider that defeat? The vehicle approached, but did not slow. Hope wilted. Then it drove right on by, and expectations were scattered by the van's passage. It zoomed by so fast that I had no chance of spying whether or not Aaron was aboard. Obviously it was going to the final expo in Altoona. I hightailed after it.

Unlike the other towns RAGBRAI had visited thus far, I was familiar with Altoona. Every Iowan, sooner or later, visits Altoona because it was home to

Adventureland. This was a medium-to-somewhat-lesser amusement park. Doc had set up at Adventureland's RV park, which he also rated as medium-to-somewhat-lesser. When I arrived he was sitting in the shade. Beside him Cheek glugged from a sweating bottle of beer.

"I see you've helped yourself to one of my cigars," I said.

Cheek replaced the sticky, mashed end of a cigar back in his mouth and chortled.

"You're chomping on it like a drill sergeant," I chided. "And here I thought you were in the Navy!"

"Congratulations!" Doc said, redirecting the conversation. "Altoona is exactly 250 miles! You're halfway done. Aaron following you?"

I plopped into a waiting chair and explained Aaron's delay. None of us were worried about his eventual return, of course. Was he not Indiana Jones? Cheek took the opportunity to take the stage.

"I had a very un-RAGBRAI-like encounter today," he began, casually regarding the saliva-soaked stub pulled from his mouth. "It was with an old man at a break spot. He was grumpy and telling everyone who would listen—whether they liked it or not—his story about how many RAGBRAIs he's done, how he got on his first one, and all those since. He was complaining about a great many things and just off the vibe."

The vibe, as Cheek put it, was something we had all noticed. We didn't remark upon it until the evenings, when Doc invariably asked about the day and we would reflect. There was a positivity that saturated every aspect of RAGBRAI, through riders, support staff, even vendors. Grumbling, as a rule, was always good-natured. Well, almost always. If someone was out of sync and genuinely negative or ugly, it was noticed right away.

Before resuming his narration, Cheek speculated, "You're going to end up just like this old man, Brian: telling your story to everyone whether they like it or not."

"Thank you," I said sarcastically. He was probably right, but I kept waiting for Doc to come to my rescue by refuting Cheek with something witty and wise. He didn't. Sigh.

"The old man was standing on my foot in line for a long, long time," Cheek continued. "I was curious to see if or when he would notice. He never did, so finally I said 'pardon me, sir, but I'll need that foot to pedal soon'. The old man turned and looked at me, upset his story was interrupted—it was the third time he was telling it—and he stalked off."

"Most un-RAGBRAI-like," I agreed.

An hour or two passed, and Aaron finally arrived. Though he'd had a long, trouble-filled day, he didn't look the worse for wear. Sipping from a beer, he told his tale.

"I didn't have long to wait for the sag wagon. The driver was in a big hurry, you see, because there was another truck he was competing with. Yes, *competing*. Apparently he felt the other guy was poaching 'official RAGBRAI business'. Adding fuel to the fire was that he was Hispanic, so our driver was throwing out all sorts of racial epithets. Shocked the hell out of me.

"The energy level in the sag wagon was really low. We all felt like we'd failed on the easiest day. To add insult to injury, we all broke down within sight of the end! I understood everyone's feelings, and shared them to a lesser degree. It all came out ugly, though, when we stopped at the roadside for another couple. Their tandem was parked upside down on the shoulder —the signal for the sag wagon—but they entered the van happy as can be. Unlike everybody else who felt failures, they were just thrilled to have access to the help they needed. Their good attitude and jokes fell amusingly flat in the tense van.

"Mostly people were just morose. The RAGBRAI vibe wasn't gone, but just flagging a bit. Nobody was angry or bitter, like our 'kindly' racial-slurring driver. He kept trying to whip everybody up into some sort of anti-immigration chant. He was Hispanic himself, I might add. Even so, he kept saying things like 'spic' and 'wetback' and all that. I guess not everyone is enlightened.

"Anyway, I was dropped off at the expo, which was a vast, hot concrete parking lot with one tiny tree. There were twenty people crowded under it because it was the only shade. As the sun crossed the sky, the crowd moved around the tree, like a long line of soldiers swinging behind the only cover when cannonballs are flying. It was hilarious. It took three hours to get my bike fixed. The good thing is that I found an air-conditioned business across the parking lot. The bad thing is it was a Jiffy Lube. There wasn't much entertainment to be found. But they were nice to let me sit in the AC. I had my iPhone so I caught up on emails and business and such.

"After, after all was said and done, after the crazy driver and the hot parking lot and the Jiffy Lube and all that, the mechanic who fixed my rim broke the fender. It was, it was like *'The...'*"

"*'The Comedy of Errors!'*" we all finished in unison.

Poor Aaron. So much for the 'easy' day!

"Aren't you worried about not looking cool with fenders on your bike?" I teased. "It's very important to look cool, Aaron."

"A stripe down the back of my work attire changed my mind on that," he replied. "But I wear a rubber band around my pant leg instead of having a chain guard. I'm fashionable that way."

I suddenly started laughing.

"You just reminded me of a little thing from my past that's been buried all these years. When I was a kid, I argued with Dad about chain guards. Oh, did I throw a fit that I couldn't take mine off. None of the cool kids had them. But after arguing and riding off in a huff, the strangest thing happened. I remember clearly it happened on 14th Avenue. Some other kids were testing a homemade bow and arrow. They shot the stupid thing at me from, like, ten feet away. The arrow was too heavy to go anywhere—made out of a metal rod, I recall—but it *did* hit my bike. And, no joke, the stupid arrow bent the chain guard into the chain. I had to remove it to ride home. Dad naturally assumed

I took it off without permission."

"To this day I'm sure Dad doesn't believe me," I finished with a chuckle. "Who would? But then again, who would make up a story like that right after arguing about it? And I was a good kid. Then again, I *was* a kid, and kids have grand imaginations."

"I rode an extra eighteen miles today," Cheek suddenly interrupted. Surprised eyes swiveled to the big guy.

"As we neared Altoona," he continued. "I was following a pretty blonde. We were talking when I noticed her turn off the designated route. I thought she knew a shortcut, so I followed her. In fact she wasn't taking a shortcut, but just riding off to a state park where her huge team is camped. I discovered this only after following her nine miles! So I had another nine miles to ride back to Altoona."

He chugged down some beer, obviously pleased with his story. And a story it was, no doubt. The announcement was a surprise to all of us, including Doc, who had spent the most time with him. When I had arrived in the very early afternoon, Cheek had already been showered and relaxed. True, he could have been very, very far ahead of us, but I doubted it.

Aaron left to shower, while Doc grilled up some meat that he, well, doctored up: bacon wrapped around filet mignon wrapped around pork tenderloin. Can't go wrong with that! Our souls were most satisfied, though in truth our bodies were more satisfied by the accompanying salad.

The boys retired earlier than ever, both being

soundly asleep before eight o'clock. Meanwhile I pawed through my selection of cigars. Their numbers were distinctly lower than expected. While I freely admit to smoking too many cigars, I hadn't sucked down nearly an entire box! The culprit was obvious, but I didn't mind. I'd brought extras to give away, after all. I had just expected to distribute them a bit more widely.

I went through the comforting ritual of preparing and lighting a cigar, while Doc sat quietly and enjoyed the night. Fireflies flitted through the sparse trees, hovering over the ungainly lay of asphalt, curbs, and grass. Some flashed brilliantly and streaked through the night like little meteors, hot on the chase of love, while others maintained a soft, casual glow in a more passive, alluring come on. Their large number brought a welcome depth and dimensionality to the otherwise flat black of night.

I pondered Cheek. Specifically I wondered why he always talked bigger stories than those around him. Part of it was just fun, of course, but I sensed something else behind it. He was not challenged by Aaron, his old friend, but he didn't know me. I suspect there lay the rub. I decided to broach the subject of Cheek's one-upmanship. Doc was one of the deepest thinkers I'd ever known, so I was curious to get his insight.

"Cheek's as good a storyteller as me," I said. "Now I know why nobody believes the crazy stuff I write about. In my case it's about outrageous foreign stuff that nobody can relate with their own experiences or corroborate. But you'll note that Cheek conveniently disappears every day. Hides the evidence, as it were."

"Oh, Cheek's different than you," Doc said. "He's not avoiding you guys so he can tell stories or anything like that. He's hiding his weakness."

"Weakness?" I asked. The word didn't seem to fit. Cheek was ungainly and out of shape, but I never thought of him as weak in any way.

"He's been in the military twenty years," Doc explained. "He needs to prove he's an alpha dog. He can't compete directly with you, so he powers away every morning to hide it. He's all about power because he needs to be. Saw it all the time in the Air Force. You should meet Aaron's grandfather. Barbara's father was a career sailor who'd seen some amazing, amazing things. He's been a part of small, highly selective military operations that directly affected the course of World War II. He was far beyond the need to show off to anyone, but even so took huge pains to hide any weakness. Yes, even from his own family. Likewise, Cheek will not show his weakness before you guys. If he feels trumped by something, he finds some way to stay on top."

I nodded into the night. I thought Doc summed it all up quite eloquently. I didn't understand machismo —self-absorbed and arrogant are different—but it did explain a great many things. Suddenly I understood why Cheek got so mad at Team Wrong on the first night. He literally wanted to fight them all! I just rarely interacted with people like that. Cheek was a military man, through and through.

And the next day, Cheek took his inner sailor to a whole new level. That night was about as smooth as riding over rumbles.

CHAPTER NINE

A Sailor in Port

I woke up very early in the morning, shivering. Creeping past a snoring Cheek, I escaped outside, where waited hot relief for chill-cramped muscles. The dark air clung wetly, and I welcomed its embrace. According to Aaron's iPhone, at this tender hour of 4:30 the humidity was already 91%. Every single county we'd ridden through in the last four days had been blaring official heat advisories, though Day 4 had been a relative reprieve. Yesterday had just missed 100 degrees on the mercury—before adjusting up for humidity, that is. Today promised a return to the *really* hot stuff.

The alarm blared 4:50AM. A hulking corpse shambled out of its cold tomb, moaning in suitable brain-hungry angst. Unfortunately brains were not readily available, so Cheek had to make do with the two remaining cowboy cookies. Despite obvious fatigue, he managed to ready his bike even as he ate a cookie, hands-free. His lips steadily brought the treat inch by inch into his greedy mouth. Meanwhile he used one hand to pump up his tires—an undeniably impressive feat of strength—while cradling the last precious cookie in the other.

Moving with the limited animation of the undead, however, Cheek failed to clip his shoes into the pedals properly. As happens to every rider sooner or later, his bike fell to the ground and took him with it. Combined man and bike collapsed in suitably zombie-like manner: in slow motion. I swear the fall took a full ten seconds. Though unable to stop the fall, Cheek did control it by rolling onto his back and holding the bike above him with his powerful legs still clipped in. On the ground he lay, wobbling comically, when suddenly a beefy arm shot up into the air. The cookie was saved!

Though the day promised heat, it was yet only humid. We set off into a faint drizzle, onto dark streets under heavy skies. As soon as we exited the town, a strong headwind tried to push us back in. I was literally shivering, but Aaron—and everyone else, really —groaned with exultation, as if the 'cold' was giving them a massage. Cheek, of course, took off ahead, no doubt to hide embarrassment over the cookie fiasco.

The hills were pretty big rollers, and, even without the strong headwind, it being the fifth day really brought our pace down. We struggled dutifully onward, skipping the first town of Mitchellville to stop for breakfast in the next town of Colfax. There were many breakfast vendors to choose from, but I was lured to one in particular.

"Ours is simply the BEST!"

I knew that voice! Sure enough, I recognized the teenage cutie with bushy brown hair fighting out of a red baseball cap as the girl from Ankeny. ANKENY! I simply had to reward her vivaciousness with my business. Maybe it was what she offered: eggs loaded with mushrooms, onions, and peppers, plus a veritable slab of breakfast sausage on a toasted English muffin. At the register they also sold 'Lady Anti-Monkey Butt' anti-friction powder. A curious pairing, that. It did not bode well.

We devoured our heavy breakfast beasts in mere moments. I immediately regretted it, feeling ten pounds heavier already. Only reluctantly did we move on, turned the first corner and lo and behold! A HUGE hill. With no momentum to tackle it we had to just deal with it: wearied, painful push after wearied, painful push.

About two-thirds of the way up the slope I had my first flat tire. Though I was not sure how I felt about it, Aaron was certainly thrilled. Perhaps the source of his joy was seeing me finally suffering a mechanical. More likely he was just pining for a 'legal' stop.

"Oh no!" came a cry from a passerby, "Kryptonite!"

I had no difficulty swapping out the tire, probably because I did it wrong. Within twenty minutes it went flat again. I speculated that while inserting the tube into the tread it had gotten pinched. Such was a common mistake, though that didn't make me feel any better about my performance. After another ten minutes—and a passerby crying 'Ah, patience, grasshopper!'—we were finally on our way.

The weather stayed in the high 80s and cloudy all morning. Excellent biking weather, were it not for the headwind. Though not as robustly, we too rushed up and down the interminable hills. The carpet of meter-high wildflowers was particularly enchanting. Entire hillsides of flowers and grasses pulsed in the wind, like the gently lapping waters of a serene pond. The biodiversity was immense. This was the 'great American desert' according to the famous, if misguided, explorer Zebulon Pike, who also called it unfarmable. Most of the day passed without further drama, a fact likely aided by Cheek's absence.

At a roadside stop somewhere near Baxter, I encountered my first pie.

I am not a pie eater by choice, but that day I discovered just how horribly, horribly wrong I was. When I finally decided to take the plunge and embrace what I'd been missing... well, it ranks as one of the very few moments of regret in my life. That slice of pecan pie was almost a religious experience. So enchanted was I that congratulating the vendor was required.

"Kelly's Berry Best Pies," I quoted to a lady beneath said banner who appeared to run the show. Her build was strong enough to say 'hard worker' and soft enough to say 'middle age'. The wind tugged at her blonde hair, revealing dark roots. In all, she had the active mom and small business owner look down pat. Her enthusiasm was obvious and genuine. "Are you the Kelly who has so enriched my heretofore miserable life?"

"I am!" she replied with a big smile. "What'd you have?"

"A slice of pecan divinity," I replied, offering up prayer hands.

"That was my grandmother's recipe," she said.

"Surely you can't bake all these pies yourself?" I prompted.

"Some vendors do," she replied. A slight grimace crossed her exuberant features, indicating a rebuke was coming. "But those are home *baked*, not home made. Huge difference."

"And to a pie novice, such as myself...?"

"Home *baked*," she explained, fists on her hips with indignation, "is when they buy boxed junk and bake it at home. You'll see lots of Sara Lee boxes out back of *those* vendors."

Her posture and tone made it clear that no such sinners would be tolerated anywhere near her vicinity. I pity the baker who tried. So emphatic was she that Aaron was lured in by her sermon.

"I have a business and take my pies very seriously," she said. "We started small, but now I'm happy to say our bakery is big and modern, back at the farm. But RAGBRAI's huge, so there's all sorts of people making pies. A lot of communities work together to keep the pies home made for RAGBRAI. It's a point of pride. Church groups gather up all the ladies they can—or men, if they have the courage to work with dozens of women—to make pies from scratch. Then they'll gather at the church and move out to specific host farms to sell them."

"I'd heard, I'd heard a rumor," Aaron said, "that Lance Armstrong got on the wrong side of the pie community. Surely he didn't expound on the virtues of boxed pie?"

Kelly laughed and made a wave of dismissal. "Oh, he's from Texas, you know. He grew up eating coconut cream pie. People love cream pies and we'd love to carry them, but the rules are very strict. It's been my experience they actually check. It's a matter of refrigeration, of course."

Though tempted to remain and eat pie until the sun set, we had to move on. At the next stop, a pleasant lakeside venue at Rock Creek State Park, Aaron and I observed a pie vendor. Almost devilishly, we snuck behind their tent to check the trash. Sure enough, we found what detectives refer to as an 'orgy of evidence': an overwhelmingly obvious pile of incriminating boxes of manufactured pies, all empty.

"'*Made in China*'," I read aloud from the four-foot mound of discards. With a low whistle, I added, "Can you imagine Kelly's sniff of disdain over *that*?"

In response, Aaron asked, "You didn't make it to my wedding rehearsal dinner, right?"

"Wow," I exclaimed. "That was one helluva segue! Let me guess: as a foodie, you got General Tso himself to make dinner?"

"There *was* no General Tso, you know," Aaron

said, laughing. "Well, not related to the dish, anyway. It's an American creation. Anyway, we let anybody come to the rehearsal dinner. I'm sorry, most of the weekend is a blur and I can't remember if you were in town yet. The point is that Mom can host some pretty amazing parties, and this was one for the ages."

"What does that have to do with 'Made in China?'"

"Let's ride, and I'll tell you quite a story."

With a couple of sharp "rider ons!" we pedaled back onto the highway.

"Mom is the best event planner in the world," Aaron began, "As you know, we had our wedding in Nevada City, which played a big part in the California Gold Rush. She wanted to incorporate our surroundings, so she organized a private event at History Hill. After the afternoon rehearsal, everybody in town, whether in the rehearsal or not, met at the train depot for drinks. The bar didn't take money, only gold nuggets. Waitresses in period costumes roamed around—you know, in Victorian dresses with garters and the whole Miss Kitty from Bonanza thing—and you had to sweet talk the 'soiled doves' to get a gold nugget. Cheek was all over it, as you can imagine, and got the second most nuggets. But even he couldn't compete with Isabel's eighty-year-old uncle."

"I could tell she was pedigreed," I complimented.

"Afterwards about seventy-five people boarded the train for the trip up History Hill for dinner. Halfway up we were robbed by bandits, guns blazing and everything. There were six bandits, some in dusters with faces hidden in handkerchiefs, or Mexicans in sombreros with ammo belts around their chests, bad teeth and everything. They won a shootout with the law then shot the train engineer and took over the locomotive. They went through the cars and stole all the heart gifts that everyone brought for Isabel. When they reached my blushing bride, they announced 'We can't steal your heart. It's already been stolen!'

"At the top we were then given a guided tour of the historic Chinese graveyard. There were countless Chinese laborers in those days, of course. They're supposed to be buried back in China, but most couldn't afford it. When learning about it all, Cheek *corrected the guide.*"

"Really?" I interrupted. "Cheek's big into Gold Rush history?"

"Not at all," Aaron explained. "Doesn't know anything about it. The guide was explaining something about a tombstone, and Cheek told him that he was wrong. The guide was like, 'what do you mean?' and Cheek said, 'The tombstone doesn't say that. It's an old, formal form of Mandarin, but it clearly says...' and he then proceeded to translate it out loud!"

"Are you kidding me?"

"No joke," Aaron said, equally impressed. "The guide was in awe. So was everybody else."

I shook my head in wonder. Not just about Cheek —I was getting used to shaking my head over *him*—but in wonder that I had the privilege of knowing these über-humans. What an amazing wedding! Mine and Aurelia's had just been in a drive-thru in Reno.

Soon something interesting and new arose to take our fevered brains off the pain of unrelenting, unrepentant hills. Not new, actually, but old—Route 66 era, to be precise. For Iowa was home to a massive Burma-Shave sign program, inspired by the nationwide ad campaign of yore. A rhyming jingle was split into numerous signs posted along the highway at intervals, providing not only entertainment across an otherwise redundant landscape, but a safety reminder as well. Anyone with even a hint of curiosity could not help but be hooked, as the jingles were sometimes devilishly clever.

'If daisies are your... favorite flower... keep pushing up... those miles per hour.' Over half of Iowa's counties were already graced with original jingles, with a goal to get all 99 counties 'signed' on, if you pardon the pun. The signs we passed, however, were homemade rhymes by RAGBRAI enthusiasts.

NEED TO CHILL?

I passed by a couple I recognized: the father and sleeping girl on the tandem, she with the huge butterfly glued to her helmet. This time they were slogging up a brutal, brutal hill. This did not bother the lass whatsoever. Like her father, she stood high upon the pedals to gain extra leverage. Unlike her father, however, she was pedaling backwards, *pretending* to exert effort!

JUST ONE MORE HILL

Plodding up the next hill was an old man who was surely the hieroglyphic for schoolteacher. He may have looked the part, but certainly didn't sound it: with every single push upon the pedals he swore viciously. I did a double-take the first time, while he yelled to the cosmos, "F*@#! F*@#! F*@#!" I thought surely I had imagined it, painting my sailor vocabulary upon him, but no, on the next hill he was even more explicit. He finally added an exasperated, "Come *on*, Iowa!"

TAKE A PILL

Many signs were cruelly deceptive, however. One read, '*next town 7 miles and 3 more hills*'. In fact there were seven monster hills, one per mile, and people were bitching up a storm. It was all good-natured griping, of course, but we were hurting! At one point I saw a fat 40-something man in a car wash, face scrunched tightly closed, arms raised high as the water pummeled his body in high-powered jets. The rippling of his belly flowed in different directions as the mechanical arm circled his body like any other Volkswagen. While no doubt adventuresome, it looked excruciatingly unpleasant. If only he had read the very next series of signs...

GET CLEAN GET WET.... NEVER FRET.... THE COLLEGE HAS LOTS OF.... SHOWERS, YOU BET!

Poor bastard. Speaking of poor bastards, Aaron's bike was yet again giving him ominous signs of rebellion.

EASE BACK.... GEAR DOWN.... YOU'RE ALMOST THERE.... GRINNELL'S THE BEST TOWN!

We coasted into Grinnell, thrilled the day's ride was over. The rollers had been really tough, despite Day 5 being only a medium-length, medium-elevation day. Aaron and I had just wanted to get it all over with, so we skipped nearly every stop offering entertainment, education, or even vending. Barring Mr. Pork Chop, of course, which was ritual sacrosanct. Thus, we arrived well ahead of the pack.

Grinnell's mechanic tent was free and clear, which gave Aaron an easy opportunity to deal with his overly amorous derailer: it refused to stop rubbing on his back wheel, despite all protestations of innocence. It was time to replace the oft-fixed rim entirely and give the old Marin County a full makeover. We dared to dream this would allow us to finish the ride without any further mechanicals. This marked the third moderately large repair for Aaron. Cheek, too, had visited the mech tent three times. I suffered an unfamiliar sense of pride at my beleaguered, green-sprayed bike.

While we waited for his bike's pampering, Aaron and I tried wandering around Grinnell a bit. *Tried*. We were feeling positively drained, and extra-credit exercise did not seem worth the effort. We estimated we were operating at about 50% of our usual strength. Tomorrow, barring too much partying tonight, we anticipated 40%, and right on down the line until we finished—or didn't finish, as the case may be. We didn't really care to dwell too much upon our bodies on Day 7!

Still, we managed to appreciate one of Grinnell's real points of pride: the Merchant's National Bank designed by architect Louis Sullivan. This was one of his famed Art Deco 'jewel-boxes', which were simple, rectangular structures boasting magnificent decorative elements. We were struck by the extravagant cartouche that encased the facade's circular window, like an exploding star caught in a web of geometry. The interior was marvelous, with stained woods softly lit by cleverly placed stained glass windows and punctuated by prowling winged lions.

Too tired to continue much beyond the bank, we crashed into a booth at a restaurant called Bourbon Street. Strange to see a robustly successful jazz and Creole place in such a small town. It was a nice foreshadowing of our ultimate goal, the Mississippi River. It also reminded me of nothing less than Mardi Gras. The crowds were so thick and raucous at Bourbon Street that our waitress, an attractive young lass with dirty blonde hair, screamed to be heard.

"I feel bad," Aaron shouted back. "We're only, we're only here for a beer! No food!"

"Thank God!," she cried. "I'm so busy I'll never make it through another ten hours of this!"

"I daresay," I shouted, "The only thing you need

more than a big tip... is a big hug!"

She nodded with an odd mix of amusement and desperation. The poor woman was obviously on the verge of tears. Though I had been merely joking, I realized that following through was not unwarranted. I patted the booth beside me invitingly. She hesitated a moment, looked about conspiratorially, then plopped into the booth. I put my arm around her quivering shoulders and gave her a squeeze. She felt frail as crumpled paper. But a smile cracked her lips, and a sudden giggle overcame her. Without a word she returned to her feet and disappeared into the crowd.

Seeing Aaron's raised eyebrow, I explained, "Pretty girls always run away when I hug them."

It was too difficult to talk and we were too tired to find a quieter place. I really wanted to have that good heart-to-heart talk with Aaron, but reality wasn't meeting my expectations. When riding, there was just too much going on. When not riding, there was too much Cheek going on. I had assumed there would be oodles of time for talk, but the week was growing shorter, opportunities slimmer. Tonight we planned on hitting the town for our first and only party night. RAGBRAI was as much about live bands and beer as it was bikes, after all. Tomorrow night, Day 6, the overnight town offered a larger variety of entertainment, being a big university town. That left only the final day, which would be dominated with logistical issues. So Aaron and I sipped our beers, uncommunicative. It wasn't a total loss, though. I got to hug the pretty waitress.

Vexing, too, was our campground. Doc had brought the RV to rest in the best spot available, beside a narrow strip of grass. Otherwise it was a world of gravel and mud. At the far end of the vast mud plain, across the maddening jumble of ruts hardened to an ankle-snapping nightmare, rose a barn the size of an airplane hangar. Corrals and fences networked outward, connecting no less than six of the large structures. Even as I watched, busses and RVs lumbered and pitched over the ruts in an arduous, ungainly, and loud manner. Greasy diesel fumes wafted over us, supplanting the stench of animals and manure with dubious benefit.

As evening settled in, so did the bugs. Every mosquito bite was strangely painful, strangely piercing, considering its proboscis was only a millimeter long. That little gem of knowledge I had retained since a 6th grade science project, wherein I also learned the proboscis sheathed four sawing blades. Such knowledge did nothing to ease the sting. Gnats also bloomed aplenty. Clouds of them hovered over muddy puddles, water-filled ditches, and sweating cyclists.

Indeed, the Hawkeye State offered all sorts of little flying and stinging nuisances. It had bees and wasps galore, from little exploratory sweat bees to tougher mud daubers, yellow jackets, and hornets. Deer ticks were a problem if you kept to the woods, each boasting the opportunity of Lyme Disease. Spiders we had aplenty, from black widows to brown recluses. Though very dangerous, most tended to stick to barns and sheds. Far more common were corn spiders. Duh. Chiggers were undoubtedly the biggest pain in the butt—quite literally. Oh, how chiggers loved Iowa's humid summers, thick forests, grassy fields, and citizen ass. Whenever you sat in the grass you were at risk of the tiny arachnids biting into you. Itch like the devil, they do, and cause more red spots than an oily teen face.

Most pervasive of all were flies. Not just common house flies, but horse flies and their brethren who targeted cows and hogs—and horses, like those right across the mud from us. Insectile reconnaissance swarms descended upon everyone, curious whether the taste of these brightly-colored and noisy newcomers was better than horse flesh.

Alas, we were too tired to escape the assault. The accumulation of over 300 miles on pedal were taking their toll. While Doc was safely ensconced in the RV with his Kindle, the three riders of Team Tire Dips sat outside and were consumed.

"We need to go inside," someone said.

"Mmph," came the answer.

A faint slapping sound followed, then a grunt. The gesture of self defense had been lethargic at best. There were many such grunts in the next half hour. The sun dropped below the woods and fields to the west, inviting a greater variety of insect life to the buffet.

"We need to go downtown to the party," someone said.

"Mmph," came the answer.

Another half hour passed. More grunts. Less slaps. We were too tired for them to be effectual. In fact, we were too tired to move at all. We did, however, manage to ogle at our neighbors. We marveled at their energy. Beside us was a large van that had been abused and welded into a makeshift RV. The abusive welders themselves whooped over a family arm wrestling contest. Dad was a bulky truck-driver type with a long, pointed goatee. He wore a faded Harley Davidson T-shirt and greasy ball cap. His competing son was similarly adorned and muscled, if as-yet lacking a beer belly. As he exerted himself against the flexing, tattooed arm of his father, his face flushed purple in the lamplight. His brother, a skinny, bookish lad, encouraged him by cantering around and shouting like crazy.

"Look at him cheer," Cheek commented with an oddly absent quality to his voice. "Desperate. Reminds me of my brother."

"Who, the skinny one?"

"Yeah," he mumbled. "Our father would challenge all three of us boys. A game like that wasn't for fun. Not ever, not with him. Wasn't the way he was raised. Our grandfather was a coal miner from Pennsylvania back in the day. He beat his wife, who never lifted a finger to challenge him. You can imagine what he did to his bully son. The apple doesn't fall far from the tree, and rural Virginia wasn't any more enlightened than coal-town Pennsylvania. Our father would actually *physically* challenge us. Wouldn't respect us 'til we beat him. Took me over twenty years..."

Cheek paused. We didn't interrupt his train of thought. I, for one, was morbidly fascinated.

"My brother never stood up to our father," he continued abruptly. "Never even tried. Too small, too scared. To this day—and he's forty years old—our father still treats him like he's a little boy. Nothing but open contempt."

Silence descended upon us.

I didn't know what Aaron thought of Cheek's admission. Perhaps such an upbringing was so alien to his own experience with Doc that he just couldn't relate. Certainly that was my case. Though feeling it inappropriate to comment, I disagreed with Cheek's belief that the apple didn't fall far from the tree. I believed very strongly that it only took one generation to step up and make things better. Though my grandfather had been an inspirational man, when in drink he would disappear for days, abandoning his wife and children. It may explain why they lived in poverty, it may not. But one thing was for sure: my father would die before he did anything like that. And, because of his example, so would his three sons.

Feeling the need to break the mulling silence, I declared, "We're getting up right now or we're staying put for the night!"

"Mmph," came the answer.

Reluctantly we walked to the shuttle RAGBRAI provided. Funny how, after all those miles cycling, the rough walk over dried, rutted mud seemed the most difficult thing of all. Our legs and butts flared here and there with cries of resistance, but soon their complaints lowered to a steady grumbling. After a jerky and noisy ten minute ride in a jam-packed bus, we were dropped off in downtown Grinnell. A strange synchronicity developed between Aaron and Cheek. Though neither spoke a word, they both gravitated down the dark street towards the same local business. Curiously, I followed.

We stepped into a fairly large, fairly empty room. Other than a greeting desk, the only decoration was an upright piano against a back wall, topped with an old-fashioned oil lamp. The walls had been painted a nondescript ecru color and were otherwise unadorned. A boring greeting room, to be sure, but the real purpose of this business was all too clear. A long line of doors led into intimate, candle-lit rooms. A few doorways were graced with silhouettes of women lounging and stretching. Inside the tiny chambers figures lay upon beds, gently moaning. My eyes swept back to the desk, desperately seeking a sign that I was not actually witnessing what I thought I was.

Slumped over the desk was a middle-aged woman in thick, sagging makeup. Her curly hair was disheveled, her dress wrinkled and streaked with sweat. Obviously the proprietress, she looked nothing short of a Madam of a cow town after a long night entertaining visiting cowboys. Upon sight of three men entering her establishment, however, she pulled herself up and strode over to the doorways. With merciless authority she demanded, "Girls! Get out here and present yourselves to these men."

But the 'girls' refused. Tired voices replied, "No more, no way!" "My hands are too sore!" Through the doorways I spied weak waves of surrender. I simply couldn't believe what I was seeing. I knew *exactly* what this place was.

"A... a brothel?" I gasped, incredulous. "*Here?*"

All eyes swiveled and leveled upon me.

Awkward silence.

Finally Aaron chuckled and said, "I think you've been in Vegas too long."

Two shadows broke from the doorways and stepped into the light, revealing firm young ladies in polo shirts and short jean shorts. Both had neck-length blond hair and could have been sisters. They looked even more exhausted than the hostess.

"Ten-minute chair massage is all I can handle," one said. The other nodded in agreement.

Understanding flooded through me, followed quickly by embarrassment. Standing up a bit straighter than necessary, I quickly said, "I'm fine. Don't worry about me. These guys need your help."

"What, me sore?" Aaron teased with a grin. Cheek merely grunted. They were led to a larger side room, where two massage chairs waited. Ten minutes later, both intrepid Tire Dips looked refreshed. Cheek appeared reluctant to leave the site of such pleasure, and sat down at the piano.

"Does this work?" he asked the proprietress. He lifted the lid to expose the keys and plinked a few notes.

"Sure," she said. "May be a bit out of tune,

though."

"Can you play the piano?" Aaron asked.

"Not so much," Cheek said, extending the pointer finger of each hand and tapping out 'chopsticks'.

"I'm hungry," I muttered, annoyed at his eternal stalling. "Can we please get something to eat?"

Suddenly Cheek ripped into the full Gershwin classic 'Rhapsody in Blue'. Instantly transformed by the music, he wiggled energetically on the seat, arms pumping, hands a blur. We were transfixed. Time stopped as the blasé chamber filled with arresting, happy notes. Massage therapists, feeble and overworked, rose from the massage beds where they lie. One by one they entered, lured by the enervating marvel so expertly plucked from the keys by Cheek's fat fingers. After finishing the full 'Rhapsody in Blue', he moved onto another piece, even more demanding.

"Rachmaninov," Aaron observed knowingly.

"Did you know he could..." I whispered in awe.

Aaron shook his head and replied, "I've learned to never underestimate Cheek."

Once finished, Cheek leapt to his feet to an earnest round of applause. Rejuvenated by his musical triumph, he bowed quickly, then marched off into the night. Aaron and I, sharing big-eyed looks, followed dumbly after.

We were all hungry, but the only food vendors in the entire town were a Pizza Hut that kept running out of pizza and a Mexican tent with a line all the way down the street. Perhaps Grinnell figured 15,000 people could dine in one of the dozen or so restaurants in town. Perhaps they should have thought that through a bit more. I wondered how our waitress from Bourbon Street was holding up. I could think of worse things than trying to get another hug. However, there was a much wiser use for our temporary burst of energy.

"I'm thinking rum," I said. "You guys have been enjoying your Templeton Rye, and it's time for my cigars to have a proper companion."

With that in mind, as well as grabbing something to eat, we entered a small grocery store. I paused by the counter to ask the attendant for a flask-sized bottle of rum.

"Screw that!" Cheek said, marching right into the booze aisle.

What followed next was maddening. Cheek behaved like nothing short of a child. He rushed excitedly towards something that caught his eye and snatched it up, only to move onto the next small, shiny object. First he pulled from the fridge a cold bottle of champagne. Upon sight of a bottle of vodka, he abandoned the bubbly on a display of beef jerky. He hefted the new bottle excitedly, eyebrows raising into his hairline, then promptly set it on the floor to run over to a bottle of Jägermeister. The green bottle was lovingly caressed before it, too, was forgotten. Twenty minutes later he had chosen five different fifth-sized bottles of hard liquor and discarded them in favor of the next one that was shinier or harsher.

"Cheek," I said, "We are already exhausted and can barely walk, and it's for tonight only."

"Yeah," he replied seriously, "That's why I'm only getting one bottle."

"But..." I began, but he was already trudging down another aisle, dragging a bottle of tequila like a caveman with his club.

"He deserves this," Aaron commented, seeing my look of exasperation. "When he's on the job he's required to have a level of focus that is beyond most of us. Let's let him play."

"Of course," I agreed. "Sailors know how to party!"

Sailors had no concept of 'morning after'. Well, they knew, but just didn't care. I, too, had been a sailor and knew that freedom was so rare and precious that you maxed out every drop. While many people understood this stereotype of the Navy, many refused to believe it of any other sailors. It was very frustrating for those of us who had plied the seas. When I worked on cruise ships, I documented tons of booze and sex. Navy stories tended to involve more booze and less sex, but that's because their ships didn't enjoy an equal number of the opposite sex. Alas, most people thought I made it all up. Or, worse, thought I was just an immature frat boy. Compared to Cheek, I was the model of restraint.

Cheek selected and discarded a wide variety of items from around the store. By the time we left, there was a jar of pickles placed beside the Lunchables, a bag of BBQ Corn Nuts nested among the moon pies, and a jug of milk hidden amongst the Twizzlers. What we left with was crackers and hummus, plus a few sealed baggies of some crappy pre-mixed drink called '*Sip-n-Go Mar-GO-rita*'. Or so we thought: after exiting with our odd assembly of this and that, Cheek revealed one other selection that had made the final cut. Like a proud father, he held up a beautiful, bouncing bottle of Jack Daniels. He even gave it a loving pat on the bottom.

We wandered through the crowd-choked streets of downtown Grinnell. A large stage had been set up at the junction of two main thoroughfares, with several whopping big projection screens and a full-on light show. Thousands of spectators—riders, supporters, and locals alike—danced to the screaming of the rock band. Most screamed themselves. It was awesome. Aaron leading, we wormed our way through the crowd for a place that struck our fancy. Cheek impatiently kept bumping into him from behind, usually because he was too busy taking a swig of whiskey to pay attention. Otherwise he continued cradling the bottle like it was a baby.

Eventually we found a curb near the back of the crowd that seemed like the place to stop. It was neither more sightly nor cleaner than anywhere else, nor offered a better view of the band. We were just too tired to keep going! We eased our sore butts onto the concrete and devoured our miscellaneous goodies. Cheek washed his down with copious amounts of Jack, whereas Aaron and I hesitantly sipped at our pre-mixed margaritas. We shared a wince, negating any need to complain of our dubious choice over the blaring music.

After about an hour it was clear Cheek had had enough sitting. It was also clear he'd had enough whiskey. He staggered to his feet with a powerful, if lopsided, surge of strength. Cheek's abrupt rearing so startled Aaron that he dropped his 'Sip-n-Go' adult beverage. It sloshed across the pavement. He couldn't have been happier.

Cheek wandered among the crowd in a strange mix of blunt force and polite deference. He was a southern boy, after all, if a drunk one. With surprising delight—and a not-so-surprising swig—Cheek entered a consignment shop. The owner had stayed open late, hoping to cash in on the RAGBRAI crowd. Unfortunately for the bookish elderly lady, we were the only ones who took advantage of it. The store was almost painfully bright after wandering the crowded night, but refreshingly quiet. The oasis of serenity was soon shattered.

Cheek's kid-in-a-candy-store excitement resumed, this time by way of trying on T-shirts and funny hats. At every new article he squealed like a teenager at the mall with her girlfriends. He was particularly fond of a burgundy tee featuring a seventies-era tennis shoe ad. He paraded around the store, openly caressing his chest and, thusly, the picture of two Charlie's Angels-like models. We couldn't help but laugh at his enthusiasm, despite embarrassment at his antics. We kept shooting glances to the owner, eyes begging for her patience. She regarded us with the disdain of a disgruntled librarian. This made us laugh even more.

Two minutes later, we were anything but amused.

We stepped back out into the noisy, crowded street, and someone stepped on Cheek's foot. Still smiling and giggly, Cheek politely apologized for being in the way. The man did not accept the apology, but rather spun on Cheek belligerently to spit with contempt, "Why don't you watch where you're going, you son of a bitch?"

The most un-RAGBRAI-like aggressor was a large man, wearing a sweaty flannel shirt and ball cap. He was outrageously drunk. The bully's great size, combined with heavy drink, obviously made him feel superior, invulnerable. He was very wrong.

In a blink Cheek was right up in the man's face, beefy fists clenched with instant rage. He wasn't intimidated in the least by the bully's great size, and struck before anyone was fully aware of what was happening. With a blurring-fast, mighty thrust to the chest, Cheek pushed the man off the curb and sent him reeling backwards into the crowd. Out of control, the bully nearly collapsed the entire cluster of his friends. With their help, he righted himself, but awkwardly.

Though stunned by the speed and force of the attack, the bully wasn't ready to give up. He screamed insults so loudly that the crowd finally took notice, even over the crushing sounds of the band. Surprised onlookers stumbled over themselves to retreat.

The bully burst forward with a beer-sloppy roar.

Body pulsing with power, Cheek readied to meet the man head on.

Fortunately, the man's friends swamped him and

pulled him back. *Un*fortunately, Aaron and I had to do the same—and were nearly unable to. Cheek was astonishingly powerful. He strained against us, eager to finish what he started. With an ease that belied the effort—Aaron and I together were not meek in size—Cheek shook free from our grip. He brushed himself off, snapped in realignment, and sniffed disdainfully at the bully.

"I gotta piss, anyway," Cheek drawled dismissively, then disappeared down the dark street.

I watched him go, astonished. The crowd swallowed the drunk and his friends, and suddenly everything was back to normal. The band rocked on; screaming guitars, screaming fans. Already forgotten was what had, for one searing instant, appeared to be an unavoidable escalation into something horrible.

Shocked by the whole thing, I turned to Aaron. He was staring off in the direction Cheek had gone. Though he seemed equally disturbed, he did not look surprised.

"What the Hell was *that*?" I finally blurted.

"Something that could have been very bad," he replied gravely. "Cheek's no stranger to brawls. He was arrested once in Mississippi for a bar fight with an off-duty cop."

"You're kidding!"

"The officer wasn't in uniform," Aaron explained. "The judge ruled that Cheek hadn't been knowledgeably assaulting an officer. But *both* men were publicly intoxicated. Rather than make a scandal, they let Cheek go. He was lucky to leave port that day."

"Some friend you have, Aaron," I said drily. "Just another good ol' southern boy. When he's not being thrown in jail, he's speaking Mandarin and playing Rachmaninov."

"I told you," Aaron said. "Never underestimate Cheek."

CHAPTER TEN

The Quest

The alarm woke me at 5AM sharp. Or, rather, 5AM blunt. That's how I felt, having retired at some unknown, but undeniably late hour. Once forced awake, I shivered so much that getting up was grudgingly welcome. Cheek did not share such sentiments. He lay sprawled upon his back atop the cot beside me, completely naked. Mercifully, he rolled over and stuffed a pillow over his head, grunting, "Mom, I don't want to go to school today."

None of us felt ready for the week's longest ride. Day 6 was a whopping 75 miles and 2,681 feet elevation gain. Those numbers were unpleasant enough, but became downright scary when one factored in another number: our moving at 40% strength. We felt it all right. We were very groggy.

And very shaggy. I rubbed my bearded face and

grimaced. Usually I wore one of those designer stubble beards, but had fallen into mountain man look. Cheek, too, was nearing beard. Comparatively, Aaron had little fuzz on his chin. His cheeks were still smooth as a baby's bottom, barring a few random hairs that looked more confused than anything else.

Outside was misty and dramatic, the sun but a tiny hint far, far away. Much nearer, shifting in darkness and vapor, lurked bulky figures. Gentle snorts identified the spies as horses. Thick fog let the night linger. With the street lamps already shut off, muffled lanes were lit by dissolved porch light from homes. It was like a ghost town; empty, waiting for life to return; patient, doubting it ever would. Damp air squashed incidental noise, aiding the sense of alone among others. We rode slowly, lost among personal reflections and dignified, centenarian mansions.

I found my mind wandering to a very different predawn ride. I weighed the solitude of my training ride, the rabbit-gut disaster. It, too, had begun so very alone. But desert quiet was different than this hush. Out there it was absolute. True, most of what made the desert quiet was absent from the farm fields, too: no cars, no construction, no machines, no music. But unlike the wastes surrounding the Nevada Test Range, *here* was life. The rustling of cornstalks. The chirp of crickets. And birds! Oh, so many birds. All waited to celebrate the glorious day ahead.

I suddenly realized how much I was going to miss this. Not the biking, oh no. But I was reminded of another man who had been driven to passion by a particularly fine morning after a long, hard slog. General Robert E. Lee once declared, "It is good that war is so terrible, otherwise we would grow too fond of it." Fortunately, my war was only with rumbles.

We pulled into a column of cyclists streaming out of town. Even now, fatigued and experienced at Day 6, I still suffered a flash of joy and excitement. It was what made RAGBRAI so special. We were part of something bigger than ourselves, something each of us wanted to be in, something smelling of both adventure and yet of home, too. It was an amazing feeling. Crotch lube was just the cherry on top—or bottom, rather. Despite being tired and sore, I felt healthier than ever. Surely it was those daily rations of Mr. Pork Chop.

Despite all such warm, fuzzy feelings, however, I still couldn't shake a lingering disappointment. I glanced at Aaron's mist-shrouded figure ahead. We were like busy roommates: sharing daily routines in close proximity, but little more. I was growing frustrated. As ever, Cheek didn't help.

"I need your help finding something," he said later that morning on the road outside of the third down, Ladora. We had already crossed nearly forty miles. "It's a tradition of mine to get a memento of the ride. It's something very particular and may be hard to find. Since we're running low on time, I need you guys' help."

"You waited until halfway through day *six* of seven to start looking?" I asked incredulously. "We've missed all week!"

As usual when confronted with such criticisms,

Cheek just shrugged.

Half an hour later we pulled into the town of Marengo. It was time for rest and breakfast. Oh, and to fulfill Cheek's 'quest'. Ugh. Upon circling the town's central square—complete with inviting shade trees, soft grass, and small-town-requisite gazebo—I was enticed by a vendor selling deep-fried peanut butter and jelly sandwiches. Deep-fried peanut butter and jelly sandwiches did not interest me so much. But what else was advertised....

"Chocolate-dipped bacon!" I cried, pointing to the truck. "I *must* have chocolate-dipped bacon."

"You're finally learning, my boy!" Cheek agreed, slapping me on the back with a crushing force he'd never use on Aaron. I took the necessary pains to hide a wince.

Every inch of the vendor van was covered with bold, brightly outlined menu items. The letters themselves argued for preeminence using color, font, and size: DEEP *FRIED* PB&J. CORNDOGS. Alligator ON A *Stick*. Chocolate Dipped BACON!

"Good morning!" Cheek called up to the open, empty window of the truck. "I'm looking for some alligator on a stick!"

A man's face emerged from the shadowy kitchen recess of the truck. He leaned over a bag of powdered sugar, greasy glasses reflecting dully and smeared in the sun. He was a giant of a man, equally large in enthusiasm.

"Comin' right up!" he exclaimed.

We watched him fiddle around in a freezer, then

pull out a portion of breaded alligator large as an ear of sweet corn. He dumped it in the fryer and watched it thrash. Thick fingers groped under his arm—an area fully revealed by his sweaty tank top—to scratch his flabby chest and underarm. It was not an appetizing sight.

"How 'bout you other fellas?" he asked while alligator churned and bubbled to golden.

"Chocolate-dipped bacon, please," I replied. "Aaron, anything?"

Like all accomplished gourmets, Aaron had an inventive sense and a willingness to experiment. Even if the results were not what he wanted, he was always satisfied with a stab at unusual food combinations. But he kept staring at the cook's corpulent arms like they were nothing less than hairy snake devils emerging from a pale, rippling mass of flesh to cavort above a lake of bubbling oil. Obviously freaked, Aaron barely managed a courteous reply. "I think, I think, I think I'll abstain at this time."

"What, no béchamel sauce?" I teased.

Despite any possible reservations about its maker, Cheek's alligator on a stick was undeniably excellent. Yes, it tasted like chicken. My dish, however, tasted nothing like I expected.

"This is fantastic!" I exclaimed, cradling the Styrofoam to-go box with its steaming contents. The main area was filled with shriveled, brittle bacon, while the pre-formed cup bubbled with hot, liquid chocolate.

The big man beamed at the compliment. Taking in a huge gulp of breath, like a whale before plunging to the depths, he proceeded to explain his story in one long, unbroken sentence.

"I was down for Fourth of July in St. Louis when this guy bought some bacon that wasn't crispy like he likes so he asked me if I could fry up his bacon and I told him 'all I've got is the deep fryer' and he said 'that's fine' so I done it for him and he said 'Oh, God, this is delicious!' and ever since I've been deep frying it and I sell the Hell out of it."

"I can see why," I said, sharing a smile with my companions over our colorful host. "It *is* delicious. For some reason, it tastes exactly like Nutella. You know the chocolate spread with hazelnuts?"

"Don't know it," he said, wiping his glasses with a grimy corner of his shirt. "But I have special chocolate you know."

"I don't doubt it," I said, eager to initiate another cetacean inhalation.

"I use a special chocolate—if you ever want to do it use the kind you dip ice cream cones in—I use that one because regular chocolate that you buy from the store tastes like crap."

His rapid-fire cadence came to a sudden halt on the last word. It was such an abrupt, crass halt that Aaron was forced to stifle a laugh. We thanked the man for a genuinely enjoyable repast, then moved on. My adventure was over. Cheek's was just beginning.

"Over here," he said, gesturing to an antique shop. We gratefully leaned our bikes against the brick wall and peered in through the window. The shop was loaded with all manner of bric-a-brac. Inside we went,

Cheek perusing for his mystery item through old dresses, costume jewelry, and an entire menagerie of porcelain cats. Not finding what he sought, he presented his quest to the proprietress.

"Good morning, ma'am," he said politely. "Perhaps you can help me find something."

"That's what I'm here for, dear," she replied lightly. The lady graced herself with over-large, pink eyeglasses and tightly coiffed hair. Her laugh lines were loose, indicating age, her padded body comfortable in a satin shift. It sparkled, as did she.

"I'm looking for a small pocket knife," he said.

"Oh, I don't deal in knives or guns," she replied, aghast at the thought. Her hands came to her face, producing a gentle ripple in age-softened arms.

"I'm not looking for a weapon or anything, ma'am," Cheek hurriedly reassured her. "On all my previous RAGBRAIs, I wanted a souvenir. It had to be small because I'm in the Navy, and I wanted it to be useful. So I began collecting little pocket knives. You know, something that fits on a keychain."

Her face pinched with effort.

"You might wanna try old Nancy," she finally said. "She's two streets down. Then I'd try that other place on the corner. If they don't have it, come back and I'll take care'a you."

Cheek thanked her and we moved on. Alas, neither of her suggestions were open at the early hour. Passing a small, over-used Ace Hardware, we gave that a look-see as well. Nothing. We returned to the original antiques shop.

"Oh, no luck?" she said upon spying us. She seemed genuinely disappointed.

"No, ma'am."

"Well, if it's not a brand name yer lookin' for..."

"I don't care about cost," Cheek clarified. "It's a tradition for me, that's all. Expensive, cheap, it's all good."

"Well, lemme make some calls," she said, picking up an old rotary telephone.

"Please, no, ma'am!" Cheek hastened to say. "It's only seven o'clock in the morning!"

"Oh, hush," she said with a dismissive wave. She began pecking and spinning numbers with a ring-heavy finger, then narrated her entire operation. "Now I know Francine who lives in Victor, the nearby town, and her husband'll know. Hmm... I wonder why she's not answerin'? Well I'll just leave a message. Francine? It's Myrtle. I've a young man here lookin' fer a small pocket knife. No, not what yer thinkin', rather sumthin' that'll fit on a keychain. Give Gertie a call, she knows that fella in Ladora who sells guns. Have him call me."

She plunked the heavy receiver down with a clatter. A lady in a baby blue dress entered the store, and Myrtle waved to her, calling, "I'll be with you in a moment. I'm helpin' this young man out right now."

"No, really," Cheek said. "Please take care of..."

But Myrtle was already on the phone again, spinning away.

"Oh, Agnes, is Bob awake? Well go get 'im out of bed, there's a nice young man who wants something.

Oh, Bob? Yeah, I'm lookin' fer a small pocket knife... no, somethin' fittin' on a keychain... no? Well, let's call Tim, over in Brooklyn. OK, what's that number again? 3-9-8..."

Myrtle then began strangely multitasking. Holding the receiver next to her ear with a shoulder, she wrote down the numbers. That was expected. But what surprised us was how she also warily eyed the new customer. Big glasses couldn't hide the brow she furrowed in concern, as if the middle-aged lady in the baby blue dress were actually Tony Soprano. Certainly she looked more innocuous than we sweaty, roguish three.

The lady lingered over a waist-high, round display case. The glass top was covered entirely by all manner of knick-knacks. When she pushed aside a cluster of earrings and little plastic cats to better view the items inside the case, Myrtle nearly dropped the phone.

The customer opened her mouth to ask something, but Myrtle instantly dropped her head down to her phone and began dialing again. She called no less than three more people. When she dialed the cell phones of RAGBRAI vendors, we all began to feel truly guilty over the undue effort.

"Please, ma'am," Cheek repeated. "Don't go to so much trouble. We'll just be on our way..."

At that moment the lady in the baby blue dress stepped forward, pointed to the round case and inquired, "Is that statuette—"

"It's *not* for sale!" Myrtle interrupted with a cry.

"I'll have time to deal with you later. I'm helping these three young men just now, thank you!"

Then, to our utter astonishment, Myrtle began downright badgering the lady. Waving the heavy receiver as if threatening her with a club, she didn't stop until the baby blue dress was shooed completely out of the store. Only then did Myrtle finally set down the phone. She carefully adjusted her glasses, gave her hair a pat, and strode from behind the counter to the round case. Inside, and barely visible beneath the jumble of stuff, were earrings, necklaces, and miscellaneous jewelry. Above all rose a distinctive porcelain figurine of a lady in a widely flaring green dress.

Finally answering our looks of shock, Myrtle indicated the figurine.

"See that?" she said, eyeing it lovingly. "That's from Germany, made almost a century ago. My mom had one of those, and see how it opens in the middle? There's a powder puff in there. Mom would always powder herself fully after her bath, once a week before church, and I always thought it was so beautiful. Always wanted one. Well, when that horrible woman wanted to buy it...! Oh!"

Myrtle leaned forward and added conspiratorially, "You know what? It's my birthday this week. I'm just gonna buy it for myself. That's OK, isn't it? I can pay the consignor what she's askin', and then it'll be mine! I can do that, can't I?"

She looked desperate for us to give her the nod, so I obliged by saying, "Yes, darlin', you go buy that for yourself!"

She hastily hid her treasure again beneath a pile of banal antiques and knick-knacks. Myrtle was the sweetest, most helpful woman ever, and the poor girl was terrified to actually admit she wanted something!

Having failed to end Cheek's quest in Marengo, we moved on. I was already a little tired of it, still resentful that he waited so long and then—as always—thrust himself upon us.

A cry of 'rider up!' rippled down the entire line of riders ahead. The flow of cyclists shifted center to accommodate a rider returning sluggishly to the road. He looked really tired and needed a long, long time to get up to speed. We were all getting tired, both physically and mentally, degenerating day by day. Cracks were beginning to show in resolve, in behavior. People moved in a parody of how they started, calling out everything they encountered reflexively, thoughtlessly, like 'painted line up!', or even the more ominous 'I see the elephant!'

But not everybody was tired. Three most impressive men shot past us like bullets. Paraplegics all, they rode low, arm-powered bikes. Their spotter, on a traditional road bike, struggled desperately to keep up with them. They all passed so fast, we were prompted to share a look among ourselves. Though we knew better, we spontaneously declared in unison, "Day riders!"

The hills rose wild, the land tightening into short, steep undulations like a blanket after a restless night.

Encircling every hill, every knob, was a large creek choked with willows and silver maples. Encircling every farm, every barn, was a small creek choked with pussy willows and cattails. We were entering the land of the Amana Colonies. This area hid moments of such beauty that nearly everyone stopped to gawk. Old red barns and brick silos were tucked into green corners, their backdrop mighty oaks—Iowa's state tree. Panting, resting riders lapped up the rustic beauty. Cameras clicked so densely one feared a swarm of crickets.

The route left highways—rural as they were—to fully explore the hidden valleys and hollows. We passed enchanting valleys of rivers snarled with sandbars and flooded woods. The centuries-old, mighty oaks were used to such wet treatment, veterans all. Bald eagles soared hypnotically along the winding rivers, occasionally flashing down to capture lunch. This was our nation's pride in action, talons flashing, free and healthy and successful. Riders by the dozen parked on the bridges to watch. I, for one, never tired of seeing a bald eagle swoop down over wild waters to catch a fish.

The land began to flatten into a vast flood plain. Forests were thick as ever and so populated by deer they could be seen even in day. Cheek glanced more and more into the surrounding woods, double-take after double-take. But it wasn't deer that had him perturbed. After a full mile of this behavior, he finally slowed down to group with us.

"Something's off, but I can't figure out what," he admitted, handsome brow furrowed in confusion.

Aaron and I shared a smile. This was the land of our youth, and we knew exactly what he had only subconsciously noticed.

"Take another look at the forest," Aaron invited.

Cheek peered again into the fully grown, deep woods. Suddenly his eyes flew open in understanding.

"The trees are all in perfect rows!" he cried.

"The Amanas cut them all down and replanted them over a century ago," Aaron explained.

The Amana Colonies were a unique and interesting part of Iowa. In 1855, a large group of Germans arrived in the area to cultivate some 26,000 prime acres in the greater Iowa River valley, building colonies linked by roads, rivers, and canals. Each of the seven colonies thrived in a religion-based communal system, where all property, resources, and responsibilities were shared. Nobody received a wage. Nobody needed one. All citizens received a home, medical care, meals, and schooling by the community. In turn they were also put to work where appropriate, be it outside in the fields or inside in the kitchens. With true German industry that applied even to this day, they all but abstained from distraction to focus on quality work. Nothing but the best came out of the Amanas: hand-woven blankets, sour pickles, smoked ham, Ashton Kutcher.

Though the communal system was abandoned generations ago, the current residents of the Colonies held true to their roots. Many still spoke German, if altered by 150 years as Americans, and superb craftsmanship remained their hallmark. I'd seen

Amana-brand refrigerators and air conditioners all over the world. Ironically, their way of keeping tradition alive was by adapting. Middle Amana's dairy had become the Old Creamery Theatre, South Amana's smokehouse a fine restaurant called The Marketplace. The Millstream Brewery, built on a canal to supply beer to all seven colonies, thankfully never went out of fashion.

Along the highway and still watching bald eagles swooping over cud-chewing cows, Aaron received a phone call from Doc. He asked to intercept us because he wanted to show us something. We met at a crossroads a few miles between colonies. After loading the bikes onto the rack of the vehicle Doc had been hauling behind the RV, he drove us up into the tiny hamlet of High Amana.

A steep hill ascended past rows of large, neatly built and immaculately maintained buildings from another era. These impressive Germanic brick structures were originally homes for several families, but now likely housed a few rich retirees. Flower gardens groaned under a load of butterflies so fat they bent stems.

Nearing the top of the hill, we were rewarded with a marvelous view across rolling forest. Angular pockets of cornstalks fit into corners, shaggy tassel tops vibrant and fully open to the humid heat. Atop the very crown of the hill rested our destination: a graveyard. Thus it was appropriate to feel like death warmed over upon exiting the car. Our muscles had locked and protested mightily any movement—and we still had 25 more miles to pedal!

"I love old cemeteries," Doc explained. "When Aaron's mom and I were newlyweds stationed in Germany, we didn't have much money. We would save our pennies by stopping in little groceries to buy local cheese, bread, and wine. Then we'd take our lunch to the nearest cemetery. Each country has a different feel to their cemeteries, but they are all quiet, peaceful, pleasant places to have lunch. We would find a bench, usually in the sun, and sit and enjoy the food and the view."

I wanted to tease Doc about how morbid that was, but his presentation was most convincing. Besides, he was right: the High Amana cemetery was staggeringly peaceful. A hedge of pine trees flanked the hill, blocking even a hush of wind. Though a place of death, it brimmed with life. A full scurry of squirrels raced around each other up the pines, their energetic scrambling oddly silent. Birds swooped between headstones marching in perfect order to the eastern slope.

"I don't want to take much of your time," Doc apologized, striding down the wide central aisle of green. "But I thought you might find this interesting. Especially you, Cheek, since you're not from the area. Amana village graveyards are fairly unique."

Doc moved lightly down a row of headstones. Each of the tall, slender markers was identical in size and even in distribution. Though some of their concrete number retained their whitewash, most had been blasted grey by sharp summers, cruel winters, and indifferent decades.

"Do you know what this code means, Doc?" I asked, gesturing to a series of numbers and letters spreading below the year of death.

"That was her age," he replied, glancing down at the indicated grave. "In German, 'J' is for years, 'M' is for months, and 'T' is for days. She was just days from her twentieth birthday when she died."

"Note the dates," Doc called to us all, gesturing broadly. "The dates progress in perfect chronological order. This is part of their communal attitude. No plots were reserved for leaders or others well-to-do. No ostentation. Doctors were buried right next to bakers. Whoever was next, was next. As a doctor myself, I find that refreshing. Too many of my colleagues focus too much on such trappings for posterity to the detriment of the people currently living."

My mind wandered to similar systems I'd visited in the world. Naturally, communism first came to mind. That had failed the globe over—just ask Aurelia what it was like growing up in *that* mess. Her family was still languishing in the aftermath, decades later. 'Peeps and homies in the hood', she would squeak. But there were other communal systems that did work, even here in the United States. The Amana Colonies succeeded for eighty years. Though, to be fair, they ended communalism because too many young people wanted out.

Yet America used a communal system to build the Panama Canal—well ahead of schedule and under budget, no less—neither the hallmark of a government program. I recalled touring the old multi-family houses, left to the Panamanians when the Canal Zone was abolished in 1979. The structures were completely dilapidated and crumbling, so much so that it was hard to imagine them new and shiny and smelling of fresh paint. I couldn't imagine living in them, nor in any communal system. I didn't want to. But that didn't mean I didn't want to learn about them.

And what a fascinating cemetery! I could think of worse places to spend eternity. Furthermore, I could think of worse neighbors than a baker. Bakers had improved my life far, far more than doctors had.

I was struck by a rare moment of my own mortality. Did I want to be buried here, in Iowa? The thought had never occurred to me. My thoughts were always abroad, to the next adventure. But that didn't mean I wanted to be *buried* abroad. Still, I was uncomfortable with the thought of going so far and ending up right where I began. I mean, I do cool stuff! I delved inside the pyramids of Giza, swung in jungles of Costa Rica, leapt into Fijian waterfalls. Can't do any of that cool stuff from a communal society! More importantly, I'd been to Dracula's house on Halloween night, which was so inspiring I even married a Romanian. OK, that was a tad oversimplified, but the point was that I'd learned home was where you made it. No, full circle wasn't what I wanted.

And yet...

With shock I realized that *this* place defined me more than all the adventures I'd done since. Those overseas trips were never really what defined me.

Whenever someone asked 'who are you?' I didn't answer, 'a globe-trotting badass'—unless she was hot. No, I always said, 'I'm from Iowa.' That wasn't from habit. That was from pride. This place was what defined me, its people, its attitude. This unusual trip home—for biking 500 miles simply could not be called usual—taught me something that traveling to fifty nations didn't. Home was where you made it because it was *inside of you all along.*

And to think I hadn't been sure I wanted to spend my vacation in Iowa—'spend', a slightly better word for 'waste'. How very foolish. I had much to learn.

"Thank you for your indulgence," Doc said as we returned to the car. All of us were in a contemplative mood as Doc drove down the hill. That is, until we returned to the crossroads.

"What?" Cheek suddenly demanded. "You're not going to drive us the last four miles to the brewery?"

Doc did not drive us to the brewery, but he met us there.

The Millstream Brewery was a wonderful spot to take a final break before the last big push of the last big day. The Beer Garden featured a nice wooden deck right on the old canal. The trough, narrow in girth but miles in length, had long since retired; ruts from skiff-hauling oxen were now home to thistle and blackberry bushes. Flowers bloomed everywhere, as did welcome shade.

Astonishingly, Cheek announced he would abstain. He ordered a home-brewed root beer. Doc bought the rest of us a mead-inspired beer. We toasted our continuing success with a clink of plastic cups.

"Steins would, steins would have been nice," Aaron mused, gazing into his cup. "But plastic is sensible, considering this honey mead has over nine percent alcohol. American macro-brews hover at five."

"*Nine* percent?" Cheek exclaimed, even as he disappeared.

Moments later he returned and slammed two cups onto the table before him. The contents did not slosh so much as ooze, like cough syrup. Cheek slammed them both, one after the other, necking hard to get the thick brew down. He adored the stuff, and ordered two more. When it was time to go, he staggered across the street to a table where two teenage girls sold beers for those on the go. That was illegal in most of the country, but the Amanas yet retained many of their own legal exceptions. Though in the shade, they still fanned themselves, hopelessly fighting the heat.

"Honey mead!" Cheek slurred.

"We only sell the lighter beers..." one brave lass protested. But Cheek ignored her, instead plunking his wretched, battered CamelBak upon the table. A half eaten burrito fell through a hole to plunk onto the table. Grease spread outward, staining the cloth.

"Fill 'er up!" he ordered brusquely, then staggered away in search of a toilet.

The girls looked at me with a mix of astonishment and indecision. I smiled reassuringly to them and— after ensuring Cheek was out of sight—withdrew the bag, thanked the girls, and filled it with Gatorade. When he returned, I handed him the backpack without a word. Drunk already, he never noticed the switch.

After a swing by the Amana blacksmith shop in search of a pocketknife—again unsuccessful—we rode through the hamlet of Homestead. After exiting this last of the Amana Colonies, we pushed onward, tackling the next wave of rolling hills. In the next town, Oxford, I separated from Aaron and Cheek to meet up with an old friend who lived there. Thus I faced alone the final stretch, slogging up some of the worst hills of the day. I was happy indeed to make it to Coralville, the overnight town. The hardest day was done! I nearly was, too.

I had agreed to meet the boys at Caribou Coffee, but it was not where I thought it was. Well, *it* was where I thought it was, but *I* wasn't where I thought I was. In the fifteen years since I'd been gone, things had changed radically. I didn't even recognize the major thoroughfares! At the main event area, I decided to ask directions. But whom to ask? There appeared to be hundreds of volunteers, directing riders every which way.

In fact, there were 500 volunteers, *not* including the 200 homeowners hosting riders. Iowa's help-your-neighbor attitude was the best in the nation. Literally: Volunteering in America, an organization that collects and analyzes data from the U.S. Census Bureau, found Iowa ranked #1 in the nation for volunteer retention, and #2 in overall volunteer rate. We're always helpful. We're not always right. The exuberant little old black lady that helped me was positively delightful—and positively wrong. Following her directions to the letter, I circled an entire mall complex and ended up right where I started.

Wandering the park in search of a different set of directions, I stumbled onto more than I bargained for: a free show!

I stared down at a young couple rolling in the grass. Both wore RAGBRAI information support shirts. They had name tags on, too. I think. It was hard to tell because they were making out. Lost in their own co-ed world, they were going at it with gusto. Yet there was an innocence to it, somehow. Compared to the vulgar, raw sex shows of Vegas—not that I knew anything about *those*—these two were delightfully wholesome. They kissed and pushed and pulled, but nothing more.

"Ahem," I said lightly. With more than a little intentional mischief, I stood right over them. I was curious how long it would take to be noticed. Kisses, rolling. A sigh, a squeak.

"*Ahem*," I repeated. With great innocence I asked, "Can you please give me directions to Caribou Coffee?"

They continued to ignore me in favor of more... interesting... pursuits.

"*AHEM!*" I finally called with great emphasis.

The impassioned tumbling paused. The young man removed his tongue from her throat and looked up, bleary-eyed and confused.

"Welcome back to Earth," I said. "Caribou Coffee?"

"Uh, that way," he said, pointing a shaky finger.

"Two blocks. Turn right and go two more."

"Thank you," I said, but he was already launching back into the stratosphere.

After meeting up with the boys at Caribou Coffee, we rode through the busy city streets to meet up with Doc. *Coral*ville was not a name one usually associated with Iowa. Perhaps that was appropriate, as it was a suburb of the University of Iowa, which was more cosmopolitan than one usually associated with Iowa.

The entire area was under rapid development and, thus bereft of sprawling fairgrounds or open land, Doc parked the RV at Walmart. Fortunately the vast concrete field was surrounded by a fairly wide strip of green, complete with soft grass and even a row of moderately-sized trees. When facing away from the bastion of untrammeled consumerism, the site wasn't so bad. I was in no position to complain anyway. My extra clothing had become undeniably funky over the last few days, and I bought a fresh set of clothes for only fifteen bucks. Speaking of funky clothing, Aaron chose this moment to produce a full-on kilt. Wanted to be fashionable for Iowa City, he claimed. Had he not been wearing a Pastafari T-shirt with it, he may have just pulled it off.

Though all of us were physically exhausted, we were strangely enervated. We moved slowly, to be sure, but with some emotional pep. We had finished the last big day—75 miles of steeply rolling hills—and had only to 'coast' down to the Mississippi over one last day. We weren't done yet, but felt as good as there. So we had enough inclination to visit a college bar or two, a damn fine bookstore called Prairie Lights, and relax over a splendid dinner at one of Iowa City's fine, modern restaurants.

When we returned to our night's parking, the sun had long since gone down. We sat on folding chairs, backs to the brightly lit sea of concrete. Our strip of grass was bordered by a street, across from which spread an upscale apartment complex. Windows darkened one after another as the night deepened.

"Tell me, Doc," Cheek said as he sipped his Templeton. "How did you transition out of the Air Force? I'm only three weeks shy and my line of work has utterly no counterpart in the civilian world."

"I'm happy to tell you my story," Doc said. "But I don't know how helpful it will be. I'm in the medical field. I presume that is not your field of expertise...?"

I leaned in. I didn't want to pry, but my curiosity had long been piqued at Cheek's line of work.

"I'm more interested in your story, sir," Cheek said.

Disappointed, but not surprised, I pulled back to Aaron, who was busy texting his wife via his ever-present iPhone.

"You know, Aaron," I said, "Cheek is a master of changing the subject of his job. He had manipulated me several times throughout the week when I asked him what he did. He always gave an answer, but designed it away from the question. He'll go on a tangent and you never realize he didn't answer your initial question. I even remember how he successfully did it when Doc asked."

"Fooling Dad isn't easy," Aaron said, impressed. "That was when Cheek got me started talking about Monterrey? Yeah, I remember. I also remember seeing a sly grin cross Dad's face."

"That's right!" I said, chuckling in sudden recollection.

"You're right about Cheek, though," Aaron continued. "Cheek *is* a lot smarter than he lets on, no doubt about it. But even he's found his match in Dad. He says he was fooled once, in like 1965 or something, but I doubt it."

The two military men moved into the RV to continue their conversation.

"Aaron, how about that celebratory cigar a little early?" I offered, "You know you've already earned it."

"Yes," Aaron said. "I think that sounds good."

The last yonder windows darkened, but we lit up. Crickets began their conversing in earnest and finally, at long last, Aaron and I did, too. No longer were we just sharing anecdotes, huffing and puffing on the road. Those are necessary to understand a person— and fun!—but sometimes you need to ask deep questions, loaded questions, such as 'Are you happy?'

As the hours slid into morning, I confirmed what I already knew. I loved this guy. This was exactly what I was hoping to get from RAGBRAI. I wanted to rekindle our friendship, to get to know him. I had expected some grand, Hollywood-like moment of clarity. But with the best of friends, you don't need such moments. You don't even need to be together. The connection is there, deeper than our limited awareness. After being apart for years, decades even, one moment of contact and it flares back to full brightness. Great friends don't need to rekindle friendship. Great friends just are.

CHAPTER ELEVEN

Between the Waters

By the end of the week, I thought I'd seen all there was to see about RAGBRAI. I'd already ridden 400 miles, what's another 60? Already six days, what's another? Though smiling in recognition of the couple I interviewed earlier, who claimed they were surprised every year, I expected no more surprises for RAGBRAI XXXIX. I was looking forward to the end of the day and the final tire-dipping ceremony; that long-elusive moment of mutual- and self-congratulations on achieving something great. But most importantly for me, I had already achieved what brought me here in the first place. I had renewed a deep connection with an old friend. The dramas were over: my mind was already on the plane back to Vegas.

But all that was premature. I was soon to witness perhaps the most amazing thing I'd ever seen in my entire life.

Though we had all retired the night before at different hours—Cheek by ten, Aaron and I well after midnight, we were all up at 4:45AM. Surprisingly, none of us felt tired. Until pumping up our tires. Muscles not happy. Or sitting on our saddles. Butts not happy. Sadly, sometimes lube is just not enough.

Everybody was riding slower, energy low but spirits high. Fatigue does funny things to people. I was reminded of a long camping trip: on the first day you put extra effort into cleanliness, whereas after a week in the wild you're eating copious amounts of dirt and just don't care. Speaking of eating dirty things—and doing things in the wild—the 'corn latrine' ritual took an amusing turn. *Of course* there are thousands of people entering the corn fields to answer the call of nature. Sometimes you gotta do what you gotta do. But one must be careful.

"I wouldn't wiggle too much," I warned a man taking care of business at a field's bushy edge. "You're peeing into nettles."

Reflexively standing up a bit straighter, he asked nervously, "What does that mean? I'm from the city."

"You brush up against stinging nettles and you'll be howling," I explained. "And not in a good way."

"Doesn't matter," he replied with a forced laugh, "Everything's been numb below the waistline for two days now."

Even Team Roadkill was getting tired. Before they had claimed fallen critters by carefully piling

Mardi Gras necklaces upon them. By Day 7 they were just throwing beads at the poor things. Around every animal was a longer and longer trail of baubles, as their aim grew progressively fatigued.

We spied two kids exiting a field, each carrying their own full cornstalk ripped from the soil. Mounting their bikes, they cried 'Evil corn fight!' and began dueling. They swerved all over the road, swinging the stalks like sabers, dirt clods flying in every direction.

"How do they have all that energy?" I marveled.

"Day riders!" we cried in unison.

"Whether that's the case or not," Aaron added, "That's how I'm gonna remember it."

Nods all around.

The first town we stopped at was called West Branch, birthplace of President Herbert Hoover. Cheek dropped his bike to the sidewalk with a clang and stumped into line for a breakfast bowl. Soon he was snarfing down a heavy mix of scrambled eggs, diced potatoes, bacon, cheese, and sausage gravy. No doubt some MSG was ladled in there, too. Hefting the Styrofoam bomb before my wide eyes, he boasted, "The thing I love about this trip is that I can eat whatever I want!"

I recalled how on Day 1 he had patted his protruding belly and said, 'The thing I love about this trip is that I can get rid of this!' I was about to tease him about it, but he was already marching away to join the biscuits and gravy line. Aaron chose to tour a winery that had opened its doors early—doors clearly labeled 'Remove thy cleats!' and 'Persons wearing bike *cleats in here will be flogged.'*

Still on the quest to find Cheek's pocketknife, we stopped at every antique shop we could find. We had a surprisingly good time doing so. I had never considered myself one to go 'antiquing', but being a lover of history helped. In one tiny shop in an even tinier back room, I was particularly struck by a painting of a clipper ship. The vessel struggled to avoid sharp rocks, sails unfurled and taut in a mighty gail. An ancient, yellowed sales tag written in well-practiced calligraphy read, *'Oil painting, 1883.'* While no provenance was provided, I knew this was exactly the kind of place where such a statement was more often true than not.

I wandered into the next chamber of miscellaneous delights, where Cheek was busy perusing. As I watched, his gloved hand went to a series of little clothbound booklets, each so slender and small as to resemble a stack of playing cards. Randomly selecting one, he carefully pulled out the brittle book. Suddenly he barked a laugh.

"Brian, check this out!" he cried. "No joke, I just pulled this out at random. Kinda freaks me out, to be honest."

"What?"

He showed me the booklet, and I began laughing, too. It was Shakespeare's *The Comedy of Errors!*

Happily, Cheek found his small pocketknife at the third antique shop. He celebrated by having a plate of pancakes. Aaron and I decided to enjoy an egg on a stick. For only one dollar, who wouldn't want an egg on a stick? Aaron was strangely intrigued by this offering, though not nearly as much as the adorable little girl in line before us. She was cute as a button, smiling and freckled, impatient to chomp into the hard-boiled treat with youthful, over-large teeth. Aaron obligingly took her picture, but was more concerned with his own egg. He took some *serious* film of it—snapping no less than four photos, all while frowning with concentration simply undue an egg on a stick.

After another few hours, we stopped in one of the final towns for a drink. We selected a locally-owned coffee house. Upon the front door was taped a large, handwritten sign indicating a special area had been designated for RAGBRAI riders. Obligingly, we walked around to the back of the establishment. A small chamber had been reluctantly cleared, then stuffed with folding tables and folding chairs. For sale was coffee from a giant urn, bottles of orange juice, and pre-packaged muffins.

"Aren't those muffins from Costco?" Cheek asked, leaning over the paltry selection. "Why are they so expensive?"

"Good enough for RAGBRAI riders," we heard someone mutter with undisguised disdain.

We blinked in surprise at the statement, but assumed we were merely mistaken. We left the undesirable room and returned to the coffee house. Upon entering, we were immediately accosted by the teller behind the counter. He was a skinny teenager with a nose ring and a half-shaved head.

"RAGBRAI riders have a separate room in the

back," he said. "Owner set it up special."

"We saw it," Aaron said. "But I don't want a regular drip coffee. I'd like to order an iced latte, please."

"There's a room in the back for your type," the youth repeated. "The owner wants to keep the business for our regular clientele, keep out the riffraff."

Aaron stared at him in shock. When the kid's words finally sank in, Aaron showed more anger than I'd ever before seen.

"What is this, the *1950s*?" he exploded indignantly. "You're segregating undesirables? *Your* type? *Riffraff?*"

The teller shied from Aaron's outburst, while Cheek and I were forced to haul Aaron out before he throttled the kid. Aaron calmed down almost immediately, but not before taking numerous photos of the odious establishment for a future online rant. We bought a beverage at a neighboring business that welcomed customers, whether cyclists or not. It was a most unwelcome intrusion of real life. We had been living the dream, starting to cruise through the dreamy existence of joy and wholesomeness. Sooner or later, reality sets in. Sooner or later, people's true colors come out.

Returning to our bikes, I stopped over some weird tracks in the sandy soil. They were everywhere, and intriguing, but I just couldn't figure out what animal had made them. For several minutes I stared, poring over fuzzy memories of Boy Scout lessons and illustrated nature guides. No matter how hard I tried, I couldn't escape the conclusion they were from a deer abducted by aliens and subjected to some sort of rearrangement procedure.

Aaron walked by and asked, 'What are you staring at?"

"These tracks," I replied, scratching my head. "There's too many to count!"

"I'd gauge there's about 20,000," Aaron replied, bemused.

"How do you figure that?"

"10,000 riders means 20,000 cleats," he explained simply. He walked away, adding to the tracks.

Duh. It was not my finest moment. I was so tired that if you'd asked me if the Earth was a planet, I'd have said 'no'. Still, when Cheek snorted I pretended that nothing had happened. Yes, true colors were coming out!

The final hours slogged onward, as did we. It was hot as ever. I recalled a tale from the first person I'd ever met who had ridden RAGBRAI. A friend of the family, she had been in her early forties when she gave it a go sometime in the 90s. Didn't make it even to the end of the first day. 'Too hot', she had said, 'Miles and hills I can handle. But this heat? No way.' While stopping at a farm for water, I heard another story of RAGBRAI past.

"I done thirty RAGBRAIs in a row 'til this year," droned a thickset, grey-haired farmer with a walrus mustache. "Glad I ain't doin' it this year. This is far and away the hottest one. Hottest one ever, I say! And I done some hot ones!"

"Yeah, right," someone muttered in the crowd of milling, sweating bodies. "Stick to your rocking chair, old man." Though not sure who in the crowd made the rude remark, I knew all too well the type. I sighed. More true colors emerging.

Unfortunately, I was used to such reactionary disbelief. When working on cruise ships, I slaved 12-15 hours a day, 7 days a week, without a day off for 10 months straight. Few believed me. When I wrote a book about it, even more scoffed. 'Just pumping up the numbers for shock value,' they'd say, or 'nobody can do that.' How ignorant! Military personnel do it all the time, deployment after deployment. So did every doctor you'd ever met, during residency. Humans could acclimate to anything—even Las Vegas! Alas, some people were simply unwilling to put faith in anyone else. And this guy was no couch potato hiding jealousy behind disdain. He had *already* shared the challenges of RAGBRAI with 10,000 others, *already* seen hundreds of 'old men' conquering RAGBRAI. Even after all that, he chose cynicism, reactionary disbelief. I chose to believe.

"You *are* a part of this one, my friend," I said to the farmer. "Thanks for opening up your home."

As we rode past the zillionth ear of corn, my thoughts drifted back to Day 1. It was so hot and so long and so hilly. Back then, seven days seemed like an excessive amount of time. I loved the idea behind this whole endeavor, but a few days would have been fine, right? But now that Day 7 was here, I wanted it to go on forever. Kind of. I needed all those long days to break free of my normal routine, to slow down and enjoy small town life. I needed all that time to get it, and I sensed I wasn't alone. Suddenly and clearly, I understood why people did this event, year after year, even decade after decade.

But that didn't mean it was easy. I listened to Aaron and Cheek check off their aches and pains. The greatest hits list was long, not like a weekly Top 40, but a year-end countdown to the number one song. The critical favorite of both was sore knees. My knees didn't hurt so much as kept reminding me that they were there. Many riders were conversing in a like manner. Talk revolved around fatigue, pains, and home. Ah, home. When that subject arose—as it had not during much of the week—focus began to waver. Fantasies of reuniting with family became dominant, or enjoying one's own bed. Mental fatigue set in. Days of heat and hills and corn and corn and corn took their toll. Crops began blurring together. Noises, too. Mistakes happened. Some amusing, some annoying.

Some deadly.

It happened fast.

Everyone began yelling 'car up!" The old chorus was so common that most of us all but ignored it. We repeated it reflexively, but with little real concern. After all, most vehicles passing the miles-long line of cyclists slowed down as a safety precaution. But not all. Some were impatient, even dangerous. A huge, beefed up Ford truck roared down the line of cyclists, scattering riders near the center line like fallen leaves.

Cries of 'car up!' were repeated, now in earnest, with indignation. A hint of swelling intensity could be discerned.

A lady unknowingly pedaled into the oncoming traffic lane.

"Car up!" "Car up!"

First came barks, then cries, then shrieks. Warnings flared with ferocity. The truck raced ever closer. The lady cyclist, exhausted and distracted, fiddled with her water bottle.

"Car up!" people yelled, now in full panic. The shift from routine to deadly serious happened in a blink. When violence intrudes upon the usual, it is searing, immediate. We all feel the shock and are immobilized by it—like the unfocused cyclist who realized too late that she was suddenly, absolutely in mortal danger.

"Look out, lady!" "*CAR UP!*"

The truck driver may have seen her, he may not have. Maybe he thought slowing from 55 mph to 40 was enough. Maybe he didn't care. Certainly he was busy staring out his side window at the passing horde of cyclists. His truck thundered downward with killing force. Might as well have been a freight train. The lady missed her chance. She was doomed to a head-on collision with death. *Real* death, final, absolute. Violent. Horrible.

Suddenly, with a burst of power that defied belief, Cheek surged out of the line of riders. He bodily slammed into the woman, bike and all, hurtling both off the road even as the truck roared past. Hot wind and gravel from the passing vehicle blasted outward, leaving us blinking, shocked. A collective gasp escaped those who witnessed the miraculous save. Most, however, had missed it entirely. Cheek had acted that fast.

Aaron and I rushed across the road and dumped our bikes to the shoulder. Gravel streamed down into the reed-filled ditch, where Cheek had already extricated himself and his bike from the lady and her bike. He stood directly before her, strong hand placed firmly on her shoulder for support. Handsome, dark eyes looked deeply into wide, dilated blues. For a full minute she wavered within Cheek's protective grasp, blinking and disoriented. The moment she regained her senses, Cheek picked up his bike, kicked a quick adjustment to its bent frame, and took off.

She watched him go, dazed and awed. The entire scene was not unlike a superhero saving the day, then disappearing. What had for one terrible moment been all too real, now was just a 'who was that masked man?' moment. It was the most incredible thing I had ever seen.

Yes, true colors were indeed revealing themselves.

At the top of the next hill, Aaron and I searched the rolling horizon for signs of Cheek. In his usual manner, he had already powered on ahead. Cheek was not one for taking bows.

"I'm not surprised," I commented to Aaron, still eyeing the far, forested hills.

"That he's gone ahead again?"

"No," I clarified. "Somehow, I'm not surprised by his amazing performance saving that woman's life. It was probably the most impressive thing I've ever seen. My mind is still trying to wrap around the dichotomy of it all."

After a moment of reflection, I continued, "You keep telling me he's 'the man' at work, and I do believe you. But all I've personally seen is inept behavior. He didn't train for a 500-mile bike ride. He didn't even put the brakes on his bike! And how many times did it break down? How many hundreds did he pay for not giving it a simple tune-up before a weeklong trek? He forgot to charge his phone, forgot to put gas in your car and stranded the bridal party on the highway. He lost your wedding rings. He gets drunk and then gets into fights. But none of that matters. When he was truly needed, he was on it."

Aaron nodded.

"That's Cheek all right," he said. "You, you know, I've always gotten the impression he wants to do something karmic. I wonder if somehow, for some reason, he feels bad about something. He's very religious, you know, kind of an old school High Anglican type."

"You think he feels guilt over something he did in the military?"

"Maybe," Aaron mused. "But I don't think so. He takes his duties very, very seriously. If he didn't believe in it, he couldn't possibly be so efficient and precise on the job."

"Which we still don't know," I observed.

"Oh, I think I do," Aaron admitted. He smiled upon sight of my jaw falling to nether regions.

"Cheek coordinates missile attacks for the Marines," Aaron explained. "If he's not precise he kills American soldiers."

"What's the big secret over that?" I asked, disappointed. "He's military. Don't they all do stuff like that?"

"Not like this," he said seriously.

Aaron glanced about, ensuring we were alone on the hilltop. "Seriously, don't tell him I said this, and it's totally unconfirmed, of course... but I'm pretty sure his real job is coordinating *nuclear* missile strikes."

I stared at Aaron in surprise. A breeze blew, tickling sweat. Each drop on my neck tingled. Finally I mumbled, "... really?"

"Totally, totally unconfirmed," Aaron repeated. "So when he's on, he's *on* in a way you can't imagine. Makes air traffic controllers look fast and loose. That's why on vacation he shuts his brain down so completely. It's his only chance to recover and balance."

I took a long moment to let the reality of the idea sink in. It was one thing to reference nuclear warheads in Hollywood thrillers, but an entirely different thing when talking about being personally responsible for evaporating countless people, real people, in the blink of an eye. Despite all the little dramas all week—Cheek's foibles, my grumbling—I knew I'd sleep better knowing a man like Cheek was on the job. Such comfort defied everything I had seen, but not everything I had learned. I chose to believe.

The National Weather Service in Davenport said ten inches of rain had fallen at the Dubuque airport by 7AM the previous day. That was only 90 miles upriver of where we were to dip our tires in the Mississippi. The storm had toppled a 50-year record—6.28 inches in July, 1961—by only *seven o'clock in the morning!* And it was still raining. In fact, they received almost 15 inches of rain that day. Las Vegas, my reluctantly adopted home, was dampened by a mere 3.5 inches per *year.*

The worldwide news media did report torrential rains—but only about elsewhere. Seoul, South Korea was making global news with their lousy 14 inches in 24 hours. Nobody cared that a larger amount of rain was flooding Iowa. Why? Because everyone on Earth just knows Iowans are tough as nails and can handle it. Duh.

The last hill of the whole RAGBRAI rose before us. Called Fairmont Hill, it was maybe 4 miles from the river—and it was big. Unlike many of the other monster inclines, however, Fairmont was populated. Houses hugged the slopes, all but stacking upon each other on their way up, up, up to the top. Driveways were full of spectators in folding chairs, sipping beer and shouting encouragement. Sprinklers were aimed into the street to shower soon-to-be-victorious riders.

About a quarter of the way up, momentum no longer aided our ascent. Gravity had easily slowed us mere mortals down, and began its inexorable pull backward. Undeterred, Aaron's face scrunched in concentration. He was going to top this last, final challenge like a man. All along his path, people raised beers high in admiration. He was very inspiring.

I, too, lowered my head in focus. I, too, wanted to hear cheers and praise. I pressed down on those spray-painted pedals for all I was worth. But I didn't hear cheers and praise. I heard a chugging snap. And laughs.

"Green machine is down!"

The chain came off the gears! Hurriedly I gripped the greasy machinery and slipped things back into place. Now, with no momentum at all, I teetered and tottered just to get started. I had conquered every single hill of the entire RAGBRAI without hitting either set of low gears, and I sure as Hell wasn't going to start on the last hill. It forced me to push down harder. It forced the chain off a second time.

Sourly, I finished the hill. It was an agonizingly slow ascent, but I kept to the highest set of gears the whole time, fulfilling my personal goal. At the top I wanted to view the grand Mississippi, see the destination that had been the subject of endless debate and fantasy. But there was no time. The hill all but disappeared beneath me, dropping downward at a whopping 10% grade, twisting and turning past houses and driveways all the way down. It was scary as Hell. My brakes were all but smoking, flecks of green paint flying everywhere.

I caught up with Aaron when the land flattened

into flood plain. We exited the density of homes and gently pedaled parallel to the Mighty Miss. A thick forest blocked our view of her. Eventually we crossed a bridge over Black Hawk Creek—poorly named, as it was a full river—just shy of where it met the Mississippi. It was grossly swollen. Indeed, the waters of the two rivers had merged into one giant morass, flooding the woods at least a meter deep, mile after mile after mile. I liked how the waters mixed. It was an apt metaphor for how all 10,000 riders flowed and merged every year at RAGBRAI. That's what this biggest bike ride in America—biggest bike ride in the world, in fact—was all about.

RAGBRAI isn't about Iowa. RAGBRAI is about people. Not just the riders, but *all* the people between the tire dips. It's about the housewives making pies, the children selling ice cream, the firemen making pancakes. It's about families opening their homes to strangers. Nor is RAGBRAI about bikes, though they are necessary. It wouldn't be the same as driving long hours through unending fields of corn. Sometimes you have to do something big, embark on a little bit of extraordinary, to connect with others. The positive vibe that saturates RAGBRAI comes from sharing that little bit of extraordinary. It comes from locals sharing their way of life, sharing what makes them happy with strangers who, as we say in Iowa, are simply friends we haven't met yet.

This amazing ride was a welcome reintroduction to what defined me. I had begun to think it was the place, but realized it was the people. Are they unique?

Not at all. Greater understanding engulfed me.

RAGBRAI isn't a ride between the Missouri and the Mississippi. We were dipping our tires in the Pacific and Atlantic. Small town Iowa is small town America. These people—*my* people—aren't all that different from anywhere else in the States. Except Las Vegas, of course. So Iowa has a lot of corn? Georgia has a lot of cotton, Idaho a lot of potatoes. What we have doesn't matter, what we do with it does. Sharing is learning. Learning is connecting. RAGBRAI is a little bit of extraordinary because we all are a little bit of extraordinary.

The sodden forest suddenly dropped away, and before us stretched the huge, grassy expanse of a riverside park. Aaron and I grinned widely and leaned in for a high five. Moments later we were pulling off our saddles—for the last time—at the back of a crowd of bikers. A large parking lot had been cleared for the masses, but riders instinctively formed up an organized line. Aaron and I didn't speak much, but rather stared at the nearby levee wall. The bloated Mississippi lapped just shy of topping it. Reports indicated it certainly would later that day. We all knew this, which explained the unspoken organization. To stall would mean to deny our following, fellow champions the privilege of ritual.

During our wait, we met up with Cheek. He peeled himself from the line ahead to join us. Doc, too, appeared, camera at the ready. The time came, and suddenly a concrete boat ramp opened before us. Tired, but hurried, we hauled our bikes into the flood-dirtied waters of the Mississippi.

Tire dipping ritual... *complete!*

Some hosts obsess with making things perfect. The perfect evening requires planning to perfection the appetizers, the drinks, the seating arrangements, the napkins, the plates, not to mention the food. They're so narrow in focus, they forget about the people they've invited.

In my case, I was so focused on reconnecting with one friend that I was slow to realize I had *10,000* friends. More, really, if you count all the fantastic local folks. I still see the fat old farmer who took the day off to fill water bottles from his garden hose and welcome everyone to Iowa. I still see the dozens of riders offering aid over every flat tire. And how could I forget the little girl with her inflated 'helping hand'? I hadn't expected those things.

Now that I had accomplished what I had expected to, I realized how limited of a goal I had set. I already knew Aaron. I already knew Iowa. Yet there was oh so much more to explore, to learn of, to be inspired by. If I had only paid attention to what I envisioned in advance, I'd be closed to all the wonders around me. I'd learn nothing.

So, *did* I learn anything? I learned that expectations are shackles.

The biggest thing I hadn't expected—not in a million years!—was Cheek. Discovering Cheek led to perhaps the greatest lesson of my life. For my RAGBRAI story wasn't about how two old friends reconnected after twenty years. It wasn't even about how expectations can be shackles. This was the story about how I learned humility.

I do cool stuff for a lot of reasons. Adventure is hardwired into me, something I can't control even if I try. My whole life has been shaped by the need to do cool stuff. It affects my every decision, from daily choices to fundamentals like how I make a living and where I do so. I wake up every morning with a burning desire to do something new, something challenging, and to share it. Doing cool stuff is my way to inspire others to maybe demand more of their own lives, more of themselves.

But then I met Cheek, and my outlook changed. By all appearances, he was a slovenly man, a grotesque. Never mind that he had a mighty brain. More to the point was that he had a mighty heart. He did cool stuff, too, but not for the reasons I did. He did it because it was his job. He did it because people needed him to. And that makes all the difference. One need not cross oceans or climb mountains to inspire others. Cheek was no bottle in the club. He was an unsung hero. Saving that woman's life was the most inspirational act I had ever witnessed.

These conclusions did not bring me down, but rather lifted me up. Cheek spent twenty years in the military training to be ready when the moment came. I could think of no better application of all my experiences than to follow his example. I knew I had it in me to be a hero, should I be called upon. Cheek showed me how. And for that reason alone, RAGBRAI was the greatest experience of my life.

I left RAGBRAI a happier, more grounded man. I had not only rekindled a dear friendship, but had rebooted my attitude, and had a fabulous time doing it. But I did leave with one question unanswered. How on Earth could I bike 500 miles and *gain* six pounds?

About the Author

Brian is the nationally best-selling and internationally award-winning author of the Cruise Confidential series—by the only American in the history of Carnival Cruise Lines to endure a full contract in the ships' restaurants. Brian's hilarious, arduous, yet inspiring journey was featured in ABC's 20/20 special, "Cruise Ship Confidential," seen by 7.61 million viewers. In fact, he's been featured on 20/20 twice, as well as The Daily Beast, BBC, and CNN.

Brian is an avid adventurer and world traveler, (50 nations and counting) from which he's brought home numerous stories and more than a few scars. Most importantly, he brought home his Romanian wife. Brian and Aurelia currently live in Las Vegas.

Also by *Brian David Bruns*
UNSINKABLE MISTER BROWN

Paris Book Festival: SILVER
London Book Festival: BRONZE
ForeWord Awards: Book of the Year
   Humor, Nominee
ForeWord Awards: Book of the Year
   Travel Essay, Nominee

"Humorous and heartfelt, this book explores the depths one man will dive to for the woman he loves. This daring spirit resonates throughout the narrative, ringing true for anyone who's ever defied his circumstances and demanded something more."
— *ForeWord Magazine*

A surprise, whirlwind romance in Romania leads Brian to chase the woman who turned his world upside down. He becomes a cruise ship waiter, an arduous existence that Bianca has born for years. The grueling hours leave them little time together, and he quickly learns that she becomes a different person at sea. With a candid, no-muss style, Bruns shows just how smitten he and Bianca are with one another, though they're not without their jokes and stubborn streaks. Beneath the playful jabs and willful tempers is a force of gravity that binds them, even when the waves get rough. But the longer he remains on the ships, the more he begins to wonder if any couple can transcend the strains of a water-logged existence.

CPSIA information can be obtained at www.ICGtesting.com
Printed in the USA
LVOW13s2201280714

396466LV00013B/312/P

9 780985 663513